The Art of Successful Service Management

Key lessons that will successfully transform the way you think about your customers

By

TONY FOON

DISCLAIMER
This publication is intended to provide helpful and informative material. The author and publisher specifically disclaim all responsibility for any liability, loss or risk, personal or otherwise, which is incurred as a consequence, directly or indirectly, from the use or application of any contents of this book. Any and all product names referenced within this book are the trademarks of their respective owners. None of these owners have sponsored, authorized, endorsed, or approved this book.

CIP catalogue record for this book is available from the Australian Library

Author: Tony Foon
Title: The Art of Successful Service Management
Cover by: Paolo F. Tiberi
Publish by: Tony Foon
ISBN: 978-1-921851-88-9
Audience: 12+
First edition: June 2020

Dedication to my wife Anne, my children Dushanka, Claude and grandson Adam, as well as to all the coaches, managers and service personnel that I had the pleasure to know and work with throughout my wonderful career.

Thank You.

CONTENTS

TESTIMONIALS

"Tony was the best trainer I've experienced at MB. He's very engaging, allowed class participation, and was very interactive with the team. He had solid content and presented very well. I would like more sessions at this pace and with his presentation and unique style. I found it informative, yet inclusive."
— Laura Broque, Sales Executive (Mercedes Benz Toorak)

"I can't imagine a better trainer. Tony made me feel so comfortable and more confident. He was fantastic! Really funny and makes everyone feel special. He's very supportive. I'll be going to work with a totally different attitude thanks so him!"
— Mathilda Jones, Service Advisor (South Coast BMW)

"I couldn't fault the course. It was an eye-opener for me! Tony demonstrates effective ways to communicate with peers and how to get your message across. Spot on course! Tony knows his stuff!"
— Alex Rice, Foreman (Hobart BMW)

"Genuine, realistic experience from Tony, who's been there and done it all before! I appreciate how Tony makes everyone else feel comfortable to openly share their ideas."
— Patrick O'Carroll, Service Manager (Auckland BMW)

"Informative program delivered by someone who has actual in-the-field experience on the subject. He was relevant, helpful, and very good. The course was well worth doing, and more people in the dealership should attend Tony's courses."
— Geoff Coates, Warranty Admin (Melbourne City JLR)

"I enjoyed the role plays. Tony was able to find out about our weaknesses and tailored them as opposed to just feeding the information."
— Will Wang, Sales Executive (Mercedes Benz Melbourne)

"A very well-organized training session. Very enjoyable and I liked the open discussion and sharing of experiences that was relevant. Got a lot out of the session. Tony is a great motivator and was helpful beyond the course. Good work."
— Sabrina Cramer, Sales Manager (SML Frontier)

"Course was fun and relevant. Tony was approachable and made subject matter easy to follow! Would recommend for all. Honestly was great! 11 out of 10."
— Kate Jayne Ohm, Service Advisor (South City Mazda)

"Tony knows his subject very well. Very informative and has a strong background in the industry. I learned a lot from his experiences in this session. Really fantastic course!"
— Lee Kei, Service Advisor (British Motors)

"Excellent trainer. Tony, thanks for your help in making this simple to understand. Highly recommended."
— Alan Fong, Sales Executive (British Motors LTD)

FOREWORD

May I be 100% honest? Most of the advice you will find online, in some books, and in training courses is outdated and often just recycled boring materials from years gone by. Over the last twenty years or so I've racked up thousands of hours through working experience and I've seen first-hand what works and what doesn't. There's an uncountable amount of misinformation out there, so here I am to set the record straight and set you up for success.

It has been a lifelong dream of mine to pursue a career in training so that I can enrich others with the knowledge I have acquired from my managerial, customer service, and leadership experience. I've also worked as a coach and trainer, and I believe I can make a real contribution to you and your company with added value, making a point of difference and leaving a positive impact daily.

I have tried to keep this book and the concepts as simple and as short as possible to allow people from all levels to relate to my messages. To some, this is a fantastic guide; to others, this is more than the basics. Either way, I believe in the Tao philosophy of "less is more," so take as much or as little as you will, but either way you will be better for having acquired the skills and knowledge and my personal experience to succeed. That is my ultimate goal for you. In the end, you will hopefully be more successful than I am in implementing the principles, some of which I have developed through my experiences and journey, while others I have adopted and use to my advantage to create my own style of leadership. My wish is that you do the same and develop your own style to be as effective as I have been.

Stop fighting and move into a position where you can grow the business and your career. Avoid procrastinating and start planning ahead. Whether you use one particular section from this book or use three, ten or almost everything, you will gain the wisdom and knowledge to move to the next level of your career, and success will follow you. You know what you need to do, you probably just need reminding- and that's what these chapters will achieve.

Having served my auto industry apprenticeship in South Africa in 1979 and completed my training at a BMW factory, I soon progressed to becoming a BMW Senior Master Technician and was later promoted to all different facets of the service department including the managerial level. I then emigrated and furthered my career with BMW in Canada. I have been actively involved with the BMW brand previously for approximately twenty-three years, five years with the Mercedes Benz and three years with the Audi brand, spending the last ten years facilitating and coaching service and sales consultants and managers spanning from my forty years in this industry internationally.

In 2006 I was elevated to the position of general service manager for the group and was responsible for seven dealerships and twelve franchises in total as well as being the dedicated Service Manager of the Audi franchise in Canberra.

In 2004, I attended the University of Canberra and the Australian Institute of Management and graduated with a Certification of Management. I have attained academic excellence in management and organizational development in theory and practices, marketing strategy, financial business, and human resources management. Both institutions have enabled me to acquire expertise in all facets of successful business administration.

In 2003, I was awarded the prestigious award, "Service Manager of the Year" for Daimler Chrysler in Australia.

My involvement in the operation of customer service over the years, combined with my experience to work aboard, has strengthened my leadership, teamwork as well as my problem-solving and decision-making abilities.

My extensive experience working within the retail business involves having excellent communication skills, an ability to take the initiative, being creative, and the ability to adapt a flexible work manner. All of these enable me to excel and assist any service manager to succeed in the role of a service management in the auto industry and for any organization. I use best practice methodologies to customize learning initiatives to help people improve their performance. My key skills and strengths are leadership development programs including employee engagement, emotional intelligence (and the bottom line), communication skills, customer service skills, work life balance, conflict resolution, and time management. My practical and interactive training sessions use real-life situations and experiences that develop initiative and resilience.

I'm talking primarily about my experiences from working in all facets of the service department as a first-year apprentice in the late 1970s to a group service manager over a span of forty years in total with prestigious brands such as BMW, Audi, and Mercedes Benz. This book has been written to capture some of that experience, although I want to make clear that I still have more to learn about the universe and the people that makes this journey so much more worthwhile and compelling, as I believe that we will never reach our destination because in the end there is no finish line. We should never stop learning. To quote Henry Ford, "Anyone who stop learning is old, whether at twenty or eighty. Anyone who keeps learning stays young."

From my experience, to be a great service manager you need to be a leader first and foremost. In the 1970s to 2000s, you could get away with strictly managing because the system was designed for you to look after the business and finances. Concepts such as lack of leadership, emotional intelligence, and empathy were unheard of. Managers were there to make money and report to their manager above them. You could get away with a lot more including firing without coaching if the attitude and skill set was inadequate to the organizational environment. The next generation of managers must be leaders, a manager who ensures you become the person people want to be around, customers who want to do business with, and employees who will enjoy working with.

My opinion is that you will choose the road to success by reading and following some of the examples and templates that I have used to be great and make this journey all worthwhile. I'm sharing my experiences with you in this book in order to show you how to be aware, for self-awareness is greatest when you have realized what you have done and reflect how you can make a difference moving forward. This book is delivered to set you up for success as well as serving as a guide. Everyone who has been in my coaching and learning environment will know that I believe that one size or style does not fit all. We're all unique human beings and therefore we have to develop our own style.

May you reap the fruits of joy and success of being a great service manager by the seeds that you will sow now to make a difference later on to others, to leave a positive impact by adding more value to your present position, and to engage in the ideas I lay out in *The Art of Successful Service Management.*

May you be blessed with goodness, greatness, and kindness and above all, success!

1

What Makes a Great Service Manager?

Who wants to be good when we can choose to be great? Don't be a good service manager; be a great service manager. Two characteristics come to mind when I consider what makes a great service manager.

Focusing primarily on the right people and the proper processes is all it takes, and this will eventually lead to profitability. The bottom line is all about growth, year on year, and the only way you can achieve this is through retail customer retention. What matters are long-term results. If you want to be sustainable in business long term, it isn't the profit you make today that counts but the profit you make tomorrow.

The service manager role continues to evolve as our industry changes. Be willing to learn from anyone, regardless of their status or position in the company or industry. One of the saddest observations I've made over the years was realizing that many people are reluctant to learn. When you're open to learning, you will succeed because you will not make the same mistake twice; it's the person who asks the question that learns the most. I regularly ask my colleagues, friends, and family what my blind spots are. My blind spots are what they are for a reason: You can't see them. Normally when you ask people this, they offer advice at the same time, which is great—it's a shortcut to growth. All it takes is a little courage and humility, and the ability to let go of your ego.

During many of my training courses, I'm asked, "What makes a great service manager and what are some of the things I should know or do to be effective?"

If I'm a new service manager, or if I'm employed at a new dealership, I consider the following points:

- Appoint an assistant service manager.
- Empower people; give them the autonomy to make decisions within their limitations.
- Have a one-on-one to determine each person's level and what your expectations are of each other moving forward.
- Coaching is a large part of your role as a service manager, so set goals and measure the results.
- Be a crocodile: look, wait, and seize opportunities.
- Remember the three R's—review, respond, and react:
  - Review (look at the people and processes, if there are any)
  - Respond (wait and analyze the situation)

- o React (act when you have the opportunity to turn perceived problems into challenges)
- Apply the SKS rule (stop, keep, start) to everything, and coach your employees to do the same.
- Always be mindful that your people are watching you; do wrong and they will too.

Developing People

One of the most important roles of any manager is to develop the skills and knowledge of your staff in order for them to perform at a high level. Every staff member needs a development plan and this plan should be developed by the manager together with the staff member. It isn't a performance appraisal, but it is linked.

Step 1: Determine training needs

Step 2: Choose a learning strategy

Step 3: Implement strategy

Step 4: Evaluate training and development

Remember, the more that people know and understand, the more likely they will move onward and upward in their work. Train and coach your people to succeed today and every day.

Summary of Success as a Great Service Manager

- Run the business like your own. Ask yourself, "If this was my business, would I do what I'm doing?"

- Reflect. Ask yourself those short yet powerful questions: *Why* (the new buzz word) and *How* (tried and true).

- Spend 15 to 20 minutes every Monday morning planning your week ahead. Planning is always the key to success!

- Wake up earlier and do a 20-minute interval plan for the day, every day: one third reading, one third planning, and one third exercising or meditating.

- You will succeed through a common sense approach. Be vigilant; common sense isn't always common practice. No one sets you up for success in life and, in this game, the few that do are few and far between.

Key Notes

- Always be willing to learn something new every day, regardless of what it is.
- Get used to asking questions as part of the coaching strategy
- Communicate religiously with your staff on a daily basis.
- Manage by walking around (MBWA).
- Run the business like your own.
- Have a succession plan ready.
- Coach your people regularly and develop them to be ready for success.

What is your biggest takeaway from this chapter?

2

The Characteristics of a Great Service Manager

The first characteristic is to be artistic, and the second is to be scientific. Without this balance, you will find the role difficult, and the profitability and success of the department will languish.

So, be artistic and take a big step forward. Use a paintbrush to create a simple painting that embraces patience and respect toward the people you lead and see the difference it makes.

Let me explain the artistic element. As I previously emphasized, the right people are your greatest assets, so why not treat them like your greatest assets? Many service managers, and those with titles, fail to do this because of their "What's in it for me?" attitude. My advice is that compassion and showing empathy toward your staff members will get you the results you want. To do so, you must perfect a skill called "manage by walking around" (MBWA), which I will discuss with you in greater detail later in the book.

However, there are three important key points I want to discuss that are related to the MBWA skill. The first is trust; the second is respect; and the third is constant connection or engagement with your people. When you show genuine interest in your people, they will show genuine interest in you.

As a young service manager, I remember my mentor telling me many years ago, "Tony, you're only as good as the people behind you, or the people you lead," which meant that I was only as good as my team at the back end. This is now the core of business and no longer considered the back end. For example, in the case of the automotive industry, recouping expenses requires another stream of income from the service and parts departments. I will go into more detail on this in a later chapter.

The second characteristic needed to be a great service manager is the ability to apply a scientific approach in your role as it relates to generating profitability for the dealership—to focus on the department processes, daily sales, expenses, and the monthly target. Finding the right balance between the two approaches can be the difference between generating a profitable or not so profitable department. People will make sacrifices for you when you have the balance right, and the secret is that your bottom line would be more attractive without you being overly processed and results driven. You would have obtained a better result with no additional effort or stress; you were merely smart about how you achieved it, so I urge you to seriously consider the right balance between the two characteristics.

To quote Jim Rohm: "In life, the more you give, the more you receive. You can't give what you don't have." In other words, the more attention and love you give your staff, the more love and attention they will give you, and the more abundance you will receive.

To give you an example, when I began my service manager position in a previous dealership, the budget for the department had already been set. Although previous results indicated that the target should have been attained, it was never reached. Using some of my techniques and simple processes, together with engaging and connecting with staff, we began to achieve targets. Eventually, at the end of the financial year we had achieved 49% above the budgeted target set in the year prior to my appointment.

How did I achieve this? I simply focused and directed my energy more on the artistic approach and less on the scientific, finding the right balance between the two characteristics—and the results fell into place. I used simple statements when I gave my state of the union speech. For example, "I'm only here to guide you, as you're all capable of managing yourselves"; "You know what to do, and if you require assistance, that's what I'm here for"; and "Let us celebrate our success together." Remember to ask if they have questions and be clear with your expectations as well as their expectations. Using your discretion as I did and applying the two characteristics in tandem with each other as shown in my above example could be the difference between success and results that aren't stellar.

Outdated characteristics of service managers for modern day society is the reason why the budget set in the above example was not achieved. Successful companies know this and make the necessary changes. Complacent companies inevitably fall behind and, in ten or twenty years, will wonder why it took them so long to get to where they originally wanted to be.

In my opinion, the key to using the scientific and artistic approach with your role involves one third of your time thinking and planning, one third of your time performing what you were hired to do, and one third of your time engaging and connecting with your staff and colleagues.

Here's a simple formula that you can use to keep these characteristics in balance. I call them the three C's: clarity, commitment, and consistency. I have always been an inquisitive person who seeks information, and therefore asking questions is my first "C." I've always embraced teamwork since my youth days playing in team sports, which is all about commitment and as a manager there must be total commitment from both side. So that's the second "C." As for the last "C," consistency, if we want to be successful, we need to raise our level of standard in what we deliver and then continue to maintain that level. If we lower our standard by being inconsistent, all the hard work will unravel. This formula would require both characteristics to work in balance with each other and could be applied to a simple task like reviewing, refining, and reinforcing the new modern-day service processes and removing the old processes that no longer apply. How you decide to apply the artistic element to the department will determine the scientific outcome, again by using your experience and instinct and not from applying a one-size-fits-all philosophy.

Key Notes

- Be artistic with a simple, common sense approach to building relationships; the old saying about treating your people right and they will treat your customer right is so true.

- Use your discretion and intuition to balance the two characteristics so they work to your advantage.

- Be mindful that there is no blanket solution to any situation; just because a certain method worked elsewhere, it might not be applicable in every situation.

- Balancing the artistic and scientific approach using the three-part one-third approach to time is key to getting the best results.

- A one-size approach isn't carved in stone; for example, if you have a balance of 40% artistic and 60% scientific on your previous dealership and you were successful, it certainly doesn't guarantee that you'll successful in the next dealership with your same formula.

- Remember, people's personalities are all different and there is no right or wrong,- learn to be adaptable to everyone and in every circumstance to be successful.

What is your biggest takeaway from this chapter?

3

Work Smarter With the Pareto Principle (80/20 Rule)

80/20
The Pareto
Principle

About 14 years ago, when I was employed as a general service manager for a large family group, I worked some pretty crazy hours. To give you an indication, there were seven dealerships and we had twelve franchises in total, so my days were mainly spent working with the service manager and the dealer principal, and I would often bring my work home. I was burning the candle at both ends, and after nearly two years in the role, I developed sharp pains down the sides of my arms, especially the right one. I was later diagnosed with a degenerative disc in my neck. The disc was protruding and interfering with the nerves running down the side of my right arm. It got so bad that it interfered with my sleep. After months of tests, surgery was deemed the only remedy. This entailed inserting a plastic disc between the vertebrae in my neck. I was then rehabilitated with physical therapy and eventually with Pilates; both aided my recovery.

I went further and decided to engage a business coach, from whom I gained wisdom in time management, personal preparation, planning, and being proactive. One of the things we ascertained was that my laptop never ran out of power, as it was always connected to the power source. Since then, when I'm required to bring my computer home from work, I deliberately leave the power cord at the office so that as soon as the power runs out, I stop work there and then to enjoy a well-deserved rest. I'm more vigilant with my health and posture today, and now work within my parameters to maintain a healthy lifestyle.

Nowadays, I always try to work according to the 80/20 Rule. An Italian economist, Vilfredo Pareto, using a mathematical formula to describe the unequal distribution of wealth in his country, created this principle in 1906. He observed that 20% of the people owned 80% of the wealth. The Pareto Principle, or Pareto's Law as it is sometimes called, can be a very effective tool to help you manage.

I'm sure you can relate to the following: 80% of your department income comes from 20% of your customers; 80% of your department issues are solved by 20% of your staff; and lastly, 80% of your department problems or concerns come from 20% of your staff. And I'm sure you understood that when I said I used 20% of my energy to achieve 80% of my results, that is simply the 80/20 rule in life.

Another huge concern I have is that people focus on the wrong things and neglect the right things. I call this "sweating the small stuff." As far as I'm concerned, life is too short to worry about things that are out of our control. When you change the way you look at those things, those things will change. A good work-life balance rule: Work smarter, not harder; learning to use your time more effectively is an important skill that every person can learn.

Time management to add more balance to your day:

- Create to-do lists.
- Prioritize your workload.
- Have regular meetings and catch-ups.
- Learn to delegate.
- Switch off your phone. Simply switch off your phone or avoid checking work emails after work. Alternatively, set aside half an hour each night to check your messages.
- Make your health a priority. Your health should always be an important part of your life. Go to sleep at a reasonable hour, choose healthy options for meals and snacks when you're at work, and take time out to exercise at least three times a week.

- Get a life. Leave the office at a reasonable time; it's all about balance.

- Work out what matters. The first rule is to be realistic about your needs and goals.

- Know your entitlements. Knowledge is power, so take advantage of it and make sure you know exactly what you're entitled to.

- Learn to say no. Learn to say no to unreasonable demands and leave the office on time. Saying no with respect is not only effective, it feels good.

- Ask for help. Letting go and learning to delegate will help you work smarter, not harder, and you can develop your leadership skills at the same time.

- Be web savvy. Don't neglect the convenience of technology. My son constantly puts pressure on me to embrace new technology to make my life easier. Use online services to pay bills and to do grocery shopping.

- Focus on end results. It's important to focus on positive outcomes as much as possible.

- Take time out for you. Keep your personal life and family time separate, and make sure you create clearly designated boundaries for work and personal tasks. Consider unplugging regularly from your laptop, email, and mobile phone so you can fully enjoy this personal time.

- Connect with your old contacts. It's very important to remember your values, how you started this journey.

Key Notes

The following are tips to get the important things done:

- Plan your week. This gives you clarity about what is important.
- Use your own style to plan what works for you. Do whatever suits your personality.
- Begin planning with the end in mind. Think about the outcome you want to achieve.
- Prepare for contingencies. Have a Plan B and, in some cases, also a Plan C.
- Last, but not least, remember this famous adage: Less is more.

What is your biggest takeaway from this chapter?

4

Manage Your Time Effectively

Let's start with a little exercise examining what we think time is worth for everyone. The first part of your focus should be to work out how much your time costs. This helps you see if you're spending your time profitably. If you work normal hours, you will have something like 200 productive days each year. If you work 7½ hours each day, this equates to 1,500 hours in yearly earnings divided by yearly dollar earnings. From these figures, calculate an hourly rate. This should give a reasonable estimate of how much your time is worth, which may be a surprisingly large amount!

Example:
- Yearly earnings is $120,000
- 7.5 hours per day X 200 productive days is 1500 days per annum
- $120000 / 1500 is $80 per hour

When you're deciding whether or not to take on a task, consider the following:
- What are the outcomes?
- Are you wasting your and your organizations resources on a low yield task?
  This is when you might consider delegating to achieve success; this is a skill that must be learned in order to manage your time more effectively.

Many people go through life satisfied with the status quo: handling the routine, not reaching their God-given potential, simply going with the flow and "living the dream." Others make hippos fly, reach their potential, and accomplish something major. Let me ask you: Which type of person do you want to be?

The two major components of time management are practice and purpose. The practice component refers to what you do with the minutes of your day. The purpose component refers to finding and knowing your purpose in life. When you manage the minutes of your life, and they fall into alignment with the purpose of your life, you get a fantastic chain reaction. This alignment can enable you to accomplish your tasks effectively, reach your goals quickly, and give you a greater sense of peace.

Quiet Time

God gave each of us a brain and a soul, but many of us don't make time to exercise them. I begin each day with a 45-minute meditation and also ask God, the universe, and Mother Earth for direction for the day. I think about my goals and projects, and I listen for new ideas. Every person must make time to think. Schedule an appointment with yourself and don't allow interruptions. You will be amazed by how clear your life's purpose as well as the quality of your life will become.

Create a Hippo Goal

The best way to accomplish a major goal is to break it down into smaller pieces, like the old saying, "How do you eat an elephant? One bite at a time." The same is true with major goals. For example, when I wrote this book, I broke the writing down into smaller pieces and into chunks. I got up an hour earlier each day and wrote what came to mind. At the end of the week, I had nearly completed a chapter. I continued on whenever I got an opportunity, until I completed the book. This process can be applied to almost any major undertaking. Focusing on the smaller parts makes any task much easier and keeps motivation high. When you reach your goals, reward yourself. If the goal is a huge one, try the 90/30/1 formula: For the next 90 days spend 30 minutes on one goal. If the goal is small, use the 30/30/1 formula: for the next 30 days, spend 30 minutes on one goal. Does that make sense? This formula works well for time management and goal setting.

Key Points

Calculating how much your time is worth helps you decide if a job is worth doing. The same can be said for my profession as a freelance trainer and consultant. If the work that requires my expertise isn't worth my time preparing and conducting, I let it go. This may seem arrogant, but I know what my time is worth. To use your time wisely, schedule effectively by planning and making time available for yourself.

Here are some benefits to scheduling your time properly:

- Understand what you can realistically achieve with your time.
- Plan to make the best use of the time available.
- Leave enough time for things you must absolutely do.
- Preserve contingency time to handle the unexpected.
- Minimize stress by avoiding over-commitment.
- Learn to delegate effectively and do what is worthwhile to you.

My five-step strategy is simple:

- Schedule on a regular basis, perhaps on a Sunday night for 15 minutes to start the following week.

- Block out important tasks. For example, if you're a manager, ensure time is allocated for coaching and reports.
- Review your to-do list, not someone else's.
- Block out appropriate contingency time (backup time).
- Use time wisely to get tasks done without interruptions, like phone calls and emails.

Some tips for managing your time effectively:

1. **Prioritize**

   Feeling overwhelmed by all you must do? Stop and think. Which items must be completed today? This doesn't include items you'd like to get done, only the items that must be completed.

2. **Be realistic**

   One way to set yourself up for panic is to plan an unrealistic amount of work. Use your common sense to recognize when you have over-scheduled.

3. **Delegate**

   A person who refuses to delegate will likely be a very busy and frustrated person. To personally handle every item is unnecessary and unwise.

4. Work efficiently

For example, make sure your electronic calendar works for you and stick with it.

5. Organize meetings wisely

The key ingredient for a good meeting is preparation. Ask yourself, "Is this meeting necessary?" and "Can the information be better presented another way?" If there is still the need for a meeting, plan it well.

6. Learn to say no!

Many people have a tough time saying no. They allow themselves to become members of every committee, even ones that are outside their talent or spiritual gift. People who can't say no quickly discover that their life is out of balance.

7. Destroy the paper monster

The best guideline for paperwork is to either file it or toss it.

8. Manage mail

Answer emails immediately. Don't read them and then let them pile up; keep your inbox clutter free.

9. Make lists

Keep a notepad handy to jot down projects as they arise, tasks that need doing, and even phone calls you need to make. At the end of the day or week, whichever is best for you, mark off the items handled.

10. Allow time for fun and surprises

Allow some time for spontaneity and fun in your life. Every now and then, do something nice for someone that is totally unexpected. Call someone and tell them how much you appreciate them.

Key Notes

Time management is an essential skill that helps you keep your work under control and helps keep stress to a minimum. Keep everything simple, because simplicity is the key to greatness. We would all love to have an extra couple of hours in every day. Seeing as that is impossible, we need to work smarter on things that have the highest priority and create a schedule that reflects our work and personal priorities.

What is your biggest takeaway from this chapter?

5
Great Customer Service Strategies

LEGEND

There is an old phrase: "customer is king" or "the customer is always right." More importantly, customers pay your salary and are also one of the reasons you're employed.

Consumers today care more about experiences, while many dealerships still focus on products that they sell. Moving forward, past success will trap these dealerships, so don't get caught up relying on the product or products that you sell or once sold.

We need to get the basis right, and this can only be achieved through communicating, exceeding customers' expectations, and being proactive in what we do constantly. Customer service has always been paramount. Sadly, some service managers don't really understand this, as their focus is on the bottom line and their "What's in it for me?" mentality. If managers don't focus on customer service and understand it, how do they coach and train their staff to be elite? Customer service is never about you; it is always about the other person, whether it's the customer or your team. If you properly coach your people and inspire them to shift their mindset toward providing excellence customer service, the profitability of the department will prosper.

It's positive experiences and accompanying "wow factors," not the product, that keep customers coming back for more, There are no bad products out there; the difference is the service you give and the moments of truth that occur. It's the journey that the customer experiences in the dealership that matters. If the journey has been a fantastic one, they will continue to support your products. Every manufacturer is working on their customer retention and loyalty program to enhance their brand. The days of quality and value still apply to the products and service that you provide, but there is another piece of the puzzle that is thrown into the equation: convenience. More specifically, I'm referring to how customer experience has changed. Apart from the product offering, there is digital technology, "what's it in for them" thinking, the desire for service right now, and so on. I'm sure you have experienced what I'm talking about. Guess what? That's not going to change, as the expectation bar has been raised.

Let's wind back the clock about 30 years to a dinner conversation. It's focused on what brand of car you drive, if you're driving a prestigious brand, and if you're happy with it. Let's fast forward to 2020. The same people are around the dinner table talking about cars, and the same questions are asked, except with a twist. Two extra questions are asked: "How is the after-sales service? Do they look after you?" This is the new trend—it's all about customer experience. Because of the huge amount of choices we have today we don't really have bad brands, only good and better ones. The after-sales department is the point of difference and must offer the customer a "wow" experience. This is the start of the customer journey and the reason why customers will keep returning to your dealership.

I believe that there are different levels of service that a customer will experience. The first one is normal or basic service, which is the minimum level of service a customer can receive. Businesses that give this service don't get much loyalty from their customer base. Examples of this would be a service station or a convenient store. Businesses that fall into this category focus primarily on doing the job. Therefore, the focus is on the business rather than the customer.

The other level of service is about expected experiences, which is how most manufacturers today try to educate their dealers and staff. Essentially, it's about treating customers with respect in order to retain customer loyalty. Businesses at this level make their customers feel comfortable, important, welcomed, and understood. In return, their customers are loyal because the business is customer focused. In the automotive world, we should deal with the customer and not the car. In other words, treating them with respect is the priority, and issues surrounding the car are secondary. I used to have service advisors constantly complaining about the customer car when it was in for repairs. My question that always baffled them until I changed their mindset was "How is the customer?" or "What did you do for the customer?" Not once was I concerned about the car. There is nothing I can do about the car, but there is something that I can do for the customer. The physiological situation is simple. If I'm empathetic toward the customer feelings and emotions and get their understanding (I used to use the term "buy in"), that's half the battle won. The other half is up to my workshop team to repair the car.

The last level I would like to elaborate is one of unexpected service and surprise. Think of the human basic needs of feeling connected, feeling secured, feeling special, and, lastly, feeling surprised is what many businesses are not doing but should be doing. Customers don't expect this level of service, as it goes above and beyond what they are used to experiencing or receiving, but when you do surprise them with a "wow" factor or element of surprise, they will remember this for a long time. It encapsulates the "wow factor" and sticks with them because they never expected this in the first place. In some industries it's called "delighting the customer" or "exceeding the customer's expectations." Businesses that give a little extra to their customers exceed their expectations and without a doubt will see opportunities to continue to grow. If you're creating customer retention and exciting them with "wow" ideas now, you will be miles ahead of the game and ahead of your competitors.

Simply, there are three things that customers desire:

- What they must have (their needs)
- What they would like to have (their wants)
- What would really thrill or excite them (delight)

As to the first item, customer satisfaction in needed in order for customers to continually return back to your dealership. Let's face it. Customers approach you because they have a need or problem they want you to solve. Secondly, customers need to feel welcome and connected. They may be feeling anxious or even foolish or ignorant, so making them feel welcome is very important.

Customers want to feel comfortable in the physical environment and they also want peace of mind. The physical environment refers to the appearance of the dealership, and the department in particular. This is largely the reason why manufacturers are branding their sites to look the part. Unfortunately, old-fashioned automotive businesses didn't pay much attention to physical comfort, which greatly affected customer perception. Physical comfort means paying attention to the design of the premises. In the past, the male would bring the vehicle into the dealership for repairs. Fast forward ten years and you'll see a shift that is trending toward female customers. Vehicles are complicated and knowing what a customer wants can be difficult to interpret. We must take the time to understand the customer by learning the art of listening—an important step toward customer satisfaction.

To ensure a customer's peace of mind, consider how you treat them and keep them informed of simple things. For example, use their name to communicate and let them know the price of the repair work, when the vehicle will be ready, or any delays that may occur.

I felt that most service managers don't spend enough time coaching their staff on selling the benefits. What amazes me is that they always push their team to sell and reach their targets, and when this isn't achieved, they wonder why. I'm aware of many service managers during my time that push their staff to sell without coaching them properly by addressing the key words. The words I'm referring to are value and benefits, and the need to sell both. Human nature will only purchase a commodity if they see the value and benefits, regardless. There is a simple model in selling called the features, function, and benefits model. The feature is referred to "what is the commodity," the function is simply "what does that commodity do or how does it work," and lastly the benefit is "what will that commodity provide or do for them." For most non-technical people, I don't want them to get caught up with the functionality; it would be more appropriate to use the feature and benefit only. It's enough to explain what it is and why they need it, and the what and how of replacing the part or providing the service that would benefit the customer. Put simply, if customers see the benefit, they will see the value automatically. A majority of customers don't care what they pay as long as they get what they pay for, which is superior customer service that satisfies their needs and wants. This is selling the value.

I want to touch on the last point about customer desire and start off by asking you as part of the service manager role, what are you doing to make the customer thrill or exciting them and delivering consistently good and reliable service? Remember that "customer is king" is paramount in keeping the repeat business and loyalty of your customers.

I will elaborate on some structure points for you to consider for your front line and serve as a reminder to deliver constantly. There are a few segments that, I believe, if done well and focus on performance, will enhance customer service skills to another level.

- Be brilliant at the basics in whatever we do time and again.
- Be genuine and make customers feel welcome.
- Take the time to listen and understand their needs.
- Always be positive and have a can-do attitude.
- Be honest and fair and show respect toward the customer.
- Be there for the customer. Remember, customer is king.
- Exceed the customers' expectations to make their experience special.
- Training and coaching may be the last point, but it's probably the most important.

Without the confidence of knowing what you know, you will not be able to perform with ease. The old saying, "you only know what you know," rings true. If you haven't implemented a training and a coaching program for your staff, then you're moving backward, not forward. Unfortunately for some people, performing the basics isn't basic, why? Because they don't understand, or haven't been shown, or have been shown incorrectly, and therefore have developed bad habits over the years.

Your role in guiding and coaching your staff is imperative as part of great customer service strategies. Good customer satisfaction doesn't just happen unless everyone in your team is on the same page and focused to deliver the service that your customer desires. This must be a high priority on your agenda when coaching them. In saying that, as a manager those priorities for your team can only come from you. You are required to always find methods and improve plans to move up a level with your staff in order to stay ahead of your competitors.

This industry, regardless of which department you're employed with, depends on referral and customer retention to grow. It is important that you ensure through your coaching and communication that your team is constantly improving their performance in the best interest of customer satisfaction and longevity of the dealership.

All customers want to feel important and not just like someone in a crowd. They would like to be treated as individuals because, as previously mentioned, their expectations have surpassed the brand alone. It's up to us to meet or exceed to the next level to retain them.

I'm excited to be part of this journey and look forward to contributing more to the industry that has given me so much as a professional. I'm passionate, dedicated, and committed to setting you up for success. So the next time you're feeling a little tired, and you don't really want to go out of your way for your customer, or when you'd rather talk than listen, or when you insist on being right at the expense of the customer relationship, I want you to stop and think and ask yourself this question: What's a good customer relationship worth?

Will your behavior today give you the result you want tomorrow? Are your actions today in alignment with what you really want in the future? Are you on track to deliver the best customer experience for all concerned? Check in with yourself and remember the *why* of business. You're in business because of the customers, not in spite of them.

Just as a reminder on basic service process this also includes:

- The initial telephone call before they arrive at the dealership.
- Effective and efficient communication when they come in for their scheduled appointment, plus the final delivery, quality control of the car and explanation of price/invoice.
- Informing them that they can return if they are not satisfied in any way, instilling confidence.

Most of us do this 99% of the time and think that we got it right, but the 1% that we don't do can and does come back to haunt us. The example I'm going to use is checking if the vehicle is clean. This involves walking away from your computer (something you should be doing anyway) and advising the customer their car has received a complimentary clean. In my experience, customers love the words "complimentary," "gratis," and "free."

We need to be motivated to take good care of our customers, even if it means a little more work and attention. When we do attend to a customer's needs we must listen carefully to decide what they want in the future. By making a special effort to give them a good experience every time, we are building their "emotional bank account" so they are more likely to come back and spend more money. They're also more likely to bring friends, and that is very valuable to a business. In addition, customers also just want to feel understood.

Key Notes

Rules for great customer service for you to reiterate with your front line:

- Do the basics right and follow the processes.
- Smile and build rapport with the customer.
- The customer is always right.
- Running regular staff meetings as a basis for communication and feedback.
- Never overlook or underestimate the importance of effective customer relations.
- Think of what "wow" factors or ideas you can do for the customer.
- Always be positive and enthusiastic.

- Be proactive; do what you say and say what you do.
- Communication must be open, honest, and prompt.
- Manage customers' expectations courteously and promptly.
- Never judge customers; everyone is different.

Like everything in life, by keeping to the basics and the three C's, you will achieve greatness and success.

"A customer is the most important visitor on our premises. He is not dependent on us. We are dependent on him. He is not an interruption in our work. He is the purpose of it."
Mahatma Gandhi

What is your biggest takeaway from this chapter?

6

How to Coach Gen Y

We all grew up in different generations; therefore our way of dealing with the outside world is different.

When it comes to Gen Y, we must remember that we are working with a generation raised with technology. So, when you tell them to wash a car or wash the workshop floor, we need to explain why. In simple terms, if they don't have the buy-in, you've lost them. I train Gen Y employees not by telling them what to do, but rather by asking them what they would do in a situation, or what they think the solution might be.

Gen Y wants the same thing that most people want: to be respected, to be stretched and to work in a fun, flexible environment with peers who value their contribution and take the time to get to know them. The big difference is how that message is delivered. That's done by more coaching, mentoring and collaboration, better feedback, more challenges, and a genuine interest in developing their potential and careers. Gen Y are not prepared to put up with a bad relationship or an unfulfilling career, and the most confident and capable of them are prepared to walk away in search of something else.

Four Things You Need to Know and Do

- Clearly understand what the Gen Y is saying.

- Learn the collaborative leadership coaching approach they respond to best.
- Benchmark their skills and agreed goals to keep them motivated.
- Keep them interested by designing a retention plan that rewards them intrinsically and extrinsically.

I worked with an assistant service manager who was promoted to the position of service manager when the position opened up. This person immediately acted as though he had been in the role for a few years: confident and experienced. However, I noticed that this person was never physically in his office. If you're never around your frontline, how can you coach your staff, let alone see what they're doing? This person would leave work early to go home and mow his lawn and took days off and time away from the dealership for long periods, either on lunch or otherwise. When I asked why the available hours were not filled, all I got were excuses about the marketing department. This suggested to me that this person didn't accept full accountability in their position and was quick to play the blame game, something that isn't on my agenda as a service manager. I'm afraid the buck stops with you as a service manager.

I also had a frontline service advisor program competition to credit the hard-working service advisors and give them the recognition they deserved. This particular person's team was in last position for all four quarters, which should have rung alarm bells for his general manager and stakeholders. Unless he and his team are the best, the service manager has work to do. One of the things I would suggest for an effective and efficient department is being there for your staff. Unless you're there for the most part, you have no idea what your staff is doing and what to coach them on.

To enable your team to think outside the square, I believe you need to coach them using my formula, "What Would Tony Foon Do?" You need to be there to assist them, coach them, and support them. I know too many service managers who play the blame game. I reiterate: You must coach and train; don't blame.

There seems to be a huge misconception that if I'm coaching someone, I'm actually telling them what to do. That was my thinking years ago when I was in my role as a service manager, and when my mentor said that I had to start coaching my staff, I thought "Are you kidding? I'm doing that already." Not until he asked me how I was doing it that he corrected me by saying that's not the way to do it. Coaching on the contrary is different to, say, sports coaching where you're made aware of a situation and told what and how to do it. You need to change to the mindset of being a coach instead of being a manager.

Ask yourself the question why bother to coach? Well the simple answer unfortunately is, without coaching you and your people will not succeed in this fast pace, competitive technology world. Coaching will continuously allow you to improve your team to become more effective in your roles. Coaching is a process of assisting people where they are now to where they want to be in future. Believe it or not, coaching benefits the person being coached as well as yourself.

Most managers don't coach because they will give you the excuse that they don't have time. I do agree that sometimes it takes time. However, if you're not showing interest in your people, do you blame your people not showing interest in you? Some of the reasons I think why many managers don't coach is they don't know how to coach or have never experienced being coached (this includes not having a mentor). Another reason is that there is no accountability, inspiration, or motivation on their part as well as the possibility of the fear of failure. I welcome the idea for the managers that have never experienced coaching, to contact me on my website at TonyFoon.com and engage in an appointment with me. I will be more than happy to discuss with you a road map pathway to follow for success.

Bear in mind that not everybody can be coached. However, a majority of people are open-minded depending on their attitude to change, and it takes an abundance of patience and time as well as effort. However, throughout my book and in my previous roles I have experienced coaching firsthand. It actually works. I enrolled in an accredited executive-coaching course at Swinburne University many years ago; this helped me immensely as a service manager. What makes coaching difficult are the personalities you're coaching, and some people don't want to change because they're comfortable and see no reason for change. I suggest you ask yourself the question, Where do you want these people to be and why?

The coaching method I use is a very simple method or model that has been around for years called the GROW model. The acronym stands for goal, reality, options, and what's next? All of them involve questions: What is the goal of this session, what is the reality, what are the options, and finally, what comes or happens next.

To reiterate, employing GROW involves a lot of patience, time, and effort on your behalf, but the rewards are worthwhile. I can share two of my experiences of how coaching has helped service advisors move to another level. The first service advisor had no previous experience on the role but progressed forward to being recognized as one of the best service advisors in the country. Paul was employed with the parts department when he first came from the U.K. to Australia. The dealership I was employed with got busier, but they had no budget to recruit an additional service advisor. I asked the parts manager if I could borrow Paul for two hours in the morning and two hours in the night and split his costs. He agreed.

I saw so much potential in this gentleman that I convince him to come over to the service department full time. He was employed as a postal driver in the U.K. and had no prior technical experience or any hospitality skills. What I view in this gentleman's personality was his kind, "can do" attitude as well as ability to grasp information. During the course of the day, Paul would approach me with questions involving the role. I set up a training agenda plan for Paul and started coaching him. Given the current circumstances at that time, you'd probably say it's easier if I told him how to do the job. You're quite correct in saying that, but coaching is about assisting the other person by asking him questions to gain clarity, seek a solution, and get the buy in.

Initially Paul would ask me a question and expect an answer, but what he got instead was a question to his question. This made him think about a question he just asked. A good coach would eventually draw the answer out of him, and when someone answers their own questions, they have just learned something new. I'm proud to say that Paul went on to achieve service advisor of the year for the brand after two years in the role with no prior experience.

Another example I would like to share with you regarding coaching is with a service advisor as well but on a very different level of coaching. Everyone is different and there is no right or wrong solutions, just different perspectives. The dealership that I started my role with many years ago had a very bad culture in the workshop. After my appointment in the role, I interviewed every staff member in the service department and asked them the golden question: What does it take to be a high-performance team? I ascertained that there was a common denominator that was brewing in the workshop that was the root cause of the problem. This gentleman was the workshop manager who was on vacation at that time. When Stuart came back from his vacation, I introduced myself and asked him what his future plans and goals were. Using the GROW method, I simply asked one-line questions and found out his goal was to be a service manager and that he didn't want to be in the workshop anymore. I progressed further to ask him what his options were based on his goal and reality. He replied in order to be a service manager he needed to be a service advisor first to understand that side of the business. He wanted to know what he had to do in order to pursue his goal. The easy choice was to promote Stuart to a service advisor position. This perfect scenario opened the door for a new workshop manager, which was in the succession plan. I trust that you can see how coaching can work in more ways than one.

In saying that, coaching with Stuart didn't just stop there because I made him a commitment that I would coach him as a service advisor due to his lack of hospitality skills and understanding of the service processes. The saving grace was that Stuart in his previous position had some fundamentals of the process. My coaching with him involved a "live" ad hoc session. What I mean is that if he had a question on the go he would come into my office. I would then ask him questions that the customer might ask him, so that he could familiarize the situation and get the answers ready for himself. Throughout my coaching with Stuart, I never gave him any answers except ultimatums and choices that he could use through my questioning techniques. I remember on certain occasions he would be so flabbergasted and nervous to call a customer due to his lack of confidence to deal with the conflict. In an event when that situation happened, I would sit him down after he presented all the facts and data to me. I continued to question him for awareness should the next occasion arise. I would call the customer on his behalf and put the phone on speaker with Stuart listening in on the conversation. Over the next few months I could see Stuart gain confidence in his newly appointed role, and he surpassed my other two "experienced" advisors in the front-line in terms of labor sales and customer satisfaction.

These are just two examples that I would like you to think about when coaching your staff on where are they now and where you would like them to be. Something to keep in mind: If you're helping them by coaching them, you're indirectly helping yourself. It's very simple to recruit experienced people. However, keep in mind that one can't change a bad attitude even if you're gifted with all the skills. Having the right attitude and training for the right skills will promote the longevity in your dealership in terms of probability and customer satisfaction.

There is much added value in coaching your staff to get them to realize their potential, and it all starts with you. Going forward, this is a technique and method that must be implemented if you're to have a high-performance team.

Key Notes

- Set clear expectations in the beginning of the coaching session.
- Hold your staff accountable for results.
- Coaching is about asking questions to gain clarity, not telling them answers.
- Evaluate and provide honest feedback on their progress and development.
- Effective communication is paramount for both parties, as it is a two-way street.
- Coaching is never about you; it is always about the other person.
- Coaching takes time, patience, and effort. Bear in mind that what you put in is what you get out.

- Explore different coaching methods and use the one method that works.
- Challenge your staff and coach them to find their own solutions.
- Set inspiring goals that will keep your staff enthusiastic.
- Inspire your staff to step up and seize opportunities.
- Lastly, have a structure but make it enjoyable and fun for both parties.

"Give a man a fish, and you feed him for a day. Teach a man to fish, and you feed him for a lifetime." ~ Lao Tzu

What is your biggest takeaway from this chapter?

7
Communication Skills

Google's dictionary defines communication as "the imparting or interchange of thoughts, opinions, or information by speech, writing, or signs." Communication skills are some of the most important skills you need to succeed in the workplace and in your position. It's also a process that must involve at least two people: a sender and a receiver. In regard to our industry, the importance of effective communication is to ensure staff that they are following the correct orders as advised by the client.

Most people think that communication is just about informing people of what is going on in our daily activities and operations. However, there are different ways to communicate, and we must allow ourselves to understand first before being understood. Communication isn't all about the verbal or written delivery of a message, but also the non-verbal, or body language.

It's important to recognize that for a message to be effective, you have to consider the type of person who is receiving the message. Different delivery methods must be used for different people. Everyone is different. This concerns not only our personalities but our learning abilities as well, and this can change the way a message is interpreted. In my experience, it's useful for you to familiarize yourself with the different personalities of your staff so you can tailor messages to each person and get the best response.

According to Albert Mehrabian's effective communication model, only 7% is what we say, 38% is how we say it, and 55% is body language in the way we communicate and deliver a message across.

An effective communicator is one who:
- Listens with intent
- Asks effective questions
- Builds rapport

Team Meetings

One of the best ways I communicate with my staff is through our scheduled weekly, bi-weekly, or even monthly meetings, depending on the size of your department and position. I'm not talking about the toolbox meeting or the five-minute conversation with your staff in the morning or during the day. For this scheduled meeting, draw up an agenda and document the proceedings. One of the most important items usually left out of these meetings is workplace health and safety. Another important item is a list of action items and who is the custodian of each.

Scheduled meetings are a testament to the department's desire for everyone to be successful and are the only way a department or dealership can be transparent. There should be a scheduled half-hour meeting every week, as this is the best way to clearly communicate with everyone.

Ensure that there is always an agenda set up prior and that the agenda must be followed. Normally a day or two prior to the meetings, I would encourage as many people to think about what they would like to achieve in that meeting. During several of my training sessions, when the question gets bought up about having meetings, I have discovered that most managers don't have regular meetings their staff. I find this appalling and disturbing. If you want your department to be efficient and effectual, this communication tool must never be ignored. However, don't have meetings for the sake of just having meetings. If there's no agenda or nothing of importance or relevant to be discussed, postpone the meeting to the following week.

But having no meetings, or limited meetings (that is, no formal meeting process), is a recipe for disaster, and your department will not move forward as it should. How else do you make sure that everyone is on the same page with the same goal or objective in mind, or at least singing out of the same hymn book? This is a huge part of changing your department from mediocre to good to great. If the meetings are infrequent, fine—but as long as there's some formal meeting process. These meetings can be held weekly, bi-weekly, or monthly. The decision is your choice based on your needs.

There are many types of meetings. One is the triangular type, where three people are involved; another is the ten-on-ten type, which is simply a toolbox meeting held every day at 10 A.M. for 10 minutes. Meetings are a great way to follow through with changes or make and take suggestions, comments and ideas with those present.

The One-on-One Meeting

Regular one-on-one meetings with each member of your staff is just as important as team meetings. It could be a coaching session, a weekly catch-up focusing on an earlier agenda, or even looking at a different process. I'm not talking about the once-a-year performance review meeting or when there is a crisis. The fundamental thing here is that you will get to know and understand each other properly through one-on-one meetings. What is a better way to work effectively than by keeping the lines of communication open and very transparent?

In my previous training role, I would catch up with my reporting line manager, who was the managing director once a week. It gave me great pleasure to not only focus on and talk about the business, but also to discuss general things that occasionally arose. Through these meetings, I found that simple ideas manifested, and we all know that simple ideas can sometimes be the best ideas.

In December 2014, a Google staff survey was conducted. One of the questions asked was to list factors that made a difference to their employment compared to anywhere else they had worked. Some of the common answers were "opportunities for career growth" and "tons of career development resources available." They also mentioned the frequent one-on-one short meetings with their managers.

I once had the opportunity to work with a pre-delivery manager during my role as a training and development manager. He was also in charge of the company's car detailing section. All the detailers reported to an assistant pre-delivery manager who reported to him. I was to show him the high costs incurred by the department and explain what the gross profit was. After I explained the financial side of the business to him, I decided that I wanted to involve his assistant manager as part of the plan. My philosophy is that once everyone has understood my goal, they can then plan their own goals to achieve their outcome. Transparency is the best way to aim for top results. Why? Simply because everyone is clear about their expectations and goals.

When the detailer understood the financials, and how his department could affect the results, he was amazed at just how inefficient his team was. They were very slow in producing and contributing to a better result. He also realized that there were more people in his department than he needed. It is incredible how a simple strategy like transparency, and having your employees understand it, can have a positive outcome for your company.

I cannot reiterate enough the importance of effective communication, which is the cornerstone of being an effective leader or manager. Having coached the pre-delivery manager through the results, he knew that he had to get more work or identify methods to start reducing costs or increasing sales. Had he known this ten years ago when he started, the result would have undoubtedly been different. The more you communicate with your staff, the more they understand, the more they know, and the more they care.

Another point I would like to emphasize is the importance of promptly returning messages, as this can make or break relationships for busy people. It also shows respect and that you're a good communicator.

The most difficult aspect of communication is the following up that you should (and could) have done but didn't. Being complacent is probably one of the greatest mistakes you can make. Always have the intention to follow up.

It can take a lot of effort to communicate well. However, it is essential to make the most of the opportunities life has to offer. So learn to communicate your ideas clearly. Communication isn't just about talking to get your message across;

you need to listen to see whether your message has been received loud and clear. We do this through the feedback process.

One key element that many forget is that you're responsible for making sure the message is communicated accurately. Always remember: The greater the clarity, the better prepared you are for the future.

Key Notes

- Pay attention to words and actions and ask questions to gain clarity.
- Ensure that you say what you mean, and mean what you say.
- Pay attention to your body language and understand feelings and emotions.
- Uses different communication styles for different people and situations.
- Uses clear language when speaking or writing.
- Check to make sure that the message is clear and has been understood.

What is your biggest takeaway from this chapter?

8
Customers for Life!

The best customer you have is the one you have right now. I don't understand why people fail to treat their current customers with respect or provide them with the best service. Too many service departments are complacent in their processes and often reluctant to change with the times; some also feel brand dependent. These are crucial mistakes and examples of short-term thinking.

I have always maintained that the quality of products we have today is high. Between the 1970s and 1990s people spoke about what a brand represented; in 2000 it was about value. Moving forward to 2015 and beyond, it is very much about convenience and the "wow factor."

A large number of customers drop out of the dealership network between the third and fourth year of their vehicle ownership. This is normally when they decide to either give their car back or lease another one. Those who keep their car will eventually decide to take their business elsewhere, perhaps to an independent workshop. This is the time you must implement a marketing plan to retain them. What matters are long-term results. It's not the profit you make today that counts but the profit you make tomorrow. The true measure isn't what you make month-on-month, but rather year-on-year.

We, as service managers, are all focused on the profitability of the department, especially when we are remunerated according to the bottom-line. What we forget is to focus on looking after the customer and retaining the customer. Don't think short term—get maximum profit now. With short-term thinking, you will lose customers and have long-term loss. I'm talking about the customer's journey from sales to service, repeating this process over and over again, and being an advocate for your dealership and brand. Think of it this way. If a customer doesn't come back, it will cost you about five times as much energy to attract a completely new customer, and if the scenario is the same as the previous one, you will never grow the department and dealership. To only focus on gaining new business means losing old customers out the back door. This is a win-lose situation and a recipe for poor or no growth.

The way to keep your old customers is to provide them with the customer service they need and want. Not only will you retain them in the long run, you will double your car park and possibly continue to increase it for years to come. Always remember that the customer isn't dependent on you at any given moment; you should be dependent on the customer if you are to survive and grow long term. The reality is that you must coach your staff with the same philosophy moving forward if everyone, including you, is to succeed.

Many years ago, in my position as the service manager of the largest dealership in the Southern Hemisphere, I made a profit that was unheard of in my first month. The reason was simple: They (my predecessor) didn't clean up their backyard. The profit wasn't coming through the front door or from new customers, and it would have been virtually impossible to increase the profitability five-fold in a month or two. So I closed the outstanding repair order from eight months back, which made the difference.

A lot of customers have come into your dealership previously but have left due to poor service or whatever the reason might be. The problem is that we all focus on the present customer and tend to forget about the customer that came in yesterday, that should and could come back tomorrow.

Just because you're fully booked, don't assume that you will make money forever. I say this for two reasons. First, nothing lasts forever; second, you should be looking at the future of the business and the only way to do that is through customer retention today. What you build today will determine the customer of tomorrow. As the saying goes, "You reap what you sow." The only true measure is you and what you have gained from previous years, that is, not what you will gain from today's business, but rather what you have retained from last year to this year and what you will take into next year. If your car park isn't growing, you're not as profitable as you should be. To me, it doesn't make sense that some manufacturers today only measure your throughputs.

They should focus on customer retention for future years and therefore measure your results ongoing.

Retention and Better Education for Our Customers

Pre-book the customer's next service at the time of the current service or any other repair job. Whether it's nine months or 12 months, record it in the system and invoice when printing out. One of the best opportunities to keep your customer coming back is at the time of collection. Explain what the cost of the next service is, especially if they've had a major service, as well as relevant details like what oils will be used and the importance of using the manufacturer's specific oil grade.

You might ask what the significance of this is. Picture your client deciding to go elsewhere for work. What do you think would happen if another mechanic found out what you charge at the dealer? They would offer to do it for less. Make a point of advising the customer of the value in bringing their car back. For instance, if their previous visit was for a major service that was charged at quite a high rate due to parts and oil, another mechanic might not know that it was a one-time occurrence.

There are so many excuses to get in touch with the customer as a reminder or follow up, and it is inexcusable not to make contact in one or more ways. Remember to use your discretion, of course. When and why you are contacting the customer must be clear in your mind.

When customers cease their business with us and begin business with our competition, several unfortunate situations result:

- We lose our business relationship that we worked so hard to create. This loss may seem insignificant at first, but over time it can prove quite damaging.

- If business goes elsewhere, we don't need to employ the people who were working on the account. Significant loss of business may result in people losing their jobs or the closing of the company.

- Former clients could share their experiences with their own clients and friends. Word travels fast in our information-based society.

Ask yourself, what does it cost to lose a long-term customer: $100, $1,000, or $10,000? Let's start with some statistics taken from a 2014 SCORE* survey in the United States:

- The least experienced employee in a business can lose more customers than can be gained by the most experienced employee.

- In the average business, for every customer who bothers to complain, there are 26 others who remain silent.

- The average wronged customer will tell 8 to 16 people, and about 10% will tell more than 20 people.

- 91% of unhappy customers will never purchase goods or services from you again.

- If you try to remedy customers' complaints, 82% to 95% of them will stay with you.
- It costs about five times as much to attract a new customer as it does to keep an existing one.

Key Notes

It is five times easier to keep a customer you have than to get a new one, so taking customer satisfaction and retention seriously should be serious business. In terms of profit, imagine what it can do. Believe it or not, increasing your customers by 5%–10% can raise the bottom line up to 80%.

Please refer to the "Great Customer Service Strategies" chapter for more information that will assist you and your service team.

*An integrated survey of Safety, Communication, Organizational Reliability, Physician & Employee Burnout and Engagement, that provides in-depth and actionable insights into organizational, clinical, and operational performance and risk.

What is your biggest takeaway from this chapter?

The Art of Successful Service Management

9

Feel the Fear and Make the Change

When you're a leader, people are always watching you. It's true that people look to their leaders and imitate what they do because they think your behavior is correct. However, whether it's right or wrong, you must consider that they will use it against you if required, for whatever the reason. People sometimes set you up for failure, so be mindful that your staff is watching when you're in your position of leadership. You may point out ways they can improve, but they will point out your weaknesses, maybe not directly to you but to people that work with you. For that very reason, you must praise your employees, give positive feedback and don't sweat the small stuff; believe me, it's only small stuff. Criticize constructively and coach with good intentions, otherwise you will fail.

Being complacent by assuming things will remain unchanged and taking things for granted are probably the biggest mistakes you will make as a service manager, or whatever department you manage. You might think that you're doing the right thing and continuing to develop, but you're doing so in the wrong sense. You will fail because you will not have the support of management, and this is a key attribute to your success. Unless you have this support, don't attempt to take on the system, you will not win.

An example I would like to share is from my current role as a facilitator in a certain market. I delivered a course and was criticized on particular aspects of it. Instead of taking the opportunity to view what the market wanted and working on strengthening the participants for that market in order to move forward, that particular person wanted to only look backward and focus on the negative. I felt that he had set me up for failure and I lost respect for him. Keep away from people like this. They only see the glass as half empty as opposed to half full.

In late 2000, I had the opportunity to work in one of the world's largest and most prestigious service departments. Senior management and the human resources department told me of specific people who had been in the company for a long time and had become complacent and overly relaxed in their position. They had not added value and had definitely not created a point of difference for the brand and dealership. I decided that new blood was the only way to turn this dealership around and started my course of action.

Everybody is interested in your plan and how you execute it, but are reluctant to assist when it comes to the crunch. People will complain, but few will actually support your cause. The sad thing is that if I had succeeded, senior management (who had previously faced this problem) would have benefited. They would have also, however, taken credit for the changes at my expense. Thinking back, as much as I hated not succeeding at times, those actions were either a lesson or a blessing. I have learnt from those ordeals, and I have moved on to better things in my life. This particular experience led me to write this book and was the catalyst for my journey as a successful learning and training coach/facilitator. I believe that everything happens for a reason. Be around people who are positive and your role (and life) will be positive too.

The Change Principle

- Don't get stuck in a rut. Change it up, if you haven't already. Change is good, change is easy, and yet thinking about change is hard. Don't think, just do it!

- Progress; take small steps. Don't aim for perfection. We will all make mistakes, including me!

- Plan and act; don't delay; don't procrastinate. You are the master of your own destiny.

When making changes, the key is to get your staff or your dealer principal to buy in. This requires researching the subject or change that you would like to implement. It almost sounds like a sales pitch, where you present the facts, features, advantages and benefits before anyone buys in. In my role as a Learning and Development person, whenever I had an idea about a certain course I wanted to implement, I spent days and sometime weeks researching and networking to ensure it would be successful before approaching my manager. There's nothing worse than having an idea and knowing that it will work only to be shut down because you don't have the facts. Hence my approach to preparing, planning, and being proactive. Remember to apply the "what's in it for me" concept to others before they buy in.

The most difficult stage is when you decide to make the change. We should all be receptive to change, but people are generally resistant, even if it's a change for the better. They may wonder why something that works needs to change. People are also reluctant to change because it's hard to give up a habit and adopt another one.

Part of this attitude stems from a reluctance to step outside one's comfort zone. Changing a habit means interrupting a routine that's been firmly established in someone's brain. That's not going to be easy or done automatically.

Three factors can influence change. The first is *belief*, which is probably the main one. You should believe that you can change and believe that it's better for you. The second is *commitment*, which requires you to be disciplined in your initial commitment and stay committed. The third is *motivation*, because only you can create an environment where you can and will change. These three factors must come from within to enable change, and that's the difficult part. Whatever the situation you're faced with, consider only making necessary changes. Don't change for the sake of change. Use a tool that measures change for and against an objective, then consider the benefits (or lack thereof).

Corporate processes are rarely challenged, regardless of whether they are right or wrong. So choose an ideal time to put your story out there. I call this self-realization, because if you have the choice to be right or be kind, choose kindness; being right is not always the right choice. You will learn that you don't always have to be right, so choose your moments. Timing is crucial to greatness.

Sometimes you have to seize an opportunity to make a change. I was only about three weeks into my role at a prestigious dealership when a certain technician, with more than 20 years of experience, threatened to resign because I decided not to enroll him on the manufacturer's master technician course. I had considered the given circumstances at the time and believed that he could not be coached. Also, there was no organizational alignment between him and the company. Prior to my appointment, this company had wanted to move him on for 10 years due to his attitude, but decided to carry him because of the legalities involved, not to mention his vast experience as a technician. To make matters worse, this technician only worked four days a week, but the company was reluctant to deal with that because the situation was difficult.

The route I took was a no-brainer. I always give people the benefit of the doubt and I seized this opportunity when it was presented. Don't ever allow anyone to hold a gun against your head. Make the call whether it's good or bad. Sometimes making a change takes raw guts and, believe me, it's not easy. I encourage you to feel the fear, make the decision and move on.

Always have a backup plan whatever you attempt to do, because not everything that you do will go according to plan. If you fail, learn from that and move on to bigger and better things. Life is full of opportunities waiting to be seized, so don't think too much about it. Do it—make the change or don't.

Fear is part of life and the key is to do something about it rather than nothing, which is the difference between successful and unsuccessful people in this world. Don't fear the mistakes you might make, rather fear the mistakes that you don't make. Sometimes the best ideas and most valuable lessons come from the mistakes that you make, and I have made a few over the years. If you're not making mistakes, you're not learning. It's as simple as that. It's okay to make mistakes, as long as no one gets hurt. Growing up with strict parents from an Asian culture, I was told that kids should be seen and not heard. I had a difficult time adapting and expressing myself, especially at a young age, socially and at school. I was always the kid who was too scared to ask questions and never said no for fear of hurting people or embarrassing myself. I'm sure many of you have been on that road and understand what I'm talking about.

Lastly, egos are a big no-no in this business and titles are cheap. In some South East Asian countries, you can buy as many manager titles as you like, cheaply. This is probably the number one reason you will fail in your current role. No one cares about how much you know until they know how much you care. Forget about that title; it means nothing to anyone if you can't perform the role diligently, with humility, and lead with compassion. Your ego will set you up for failure. I advise you to make the change now if you think you're the reason your employees are there. Don't wait. Sadly, I know only too many service managers who have huge egos and are on a heavy ego trip because of their title of service manager or general service manager. Unfortunately, half of them don't have any idea about empathy and compassion, or are completely out of touch with the real world, that is, when it comes to leading and performing their role diligently.

Here are some examples of other managers leading with their egos, which I experienced when working as a service manager:

- I have been employed at various dealerships where department managers hold their titles in high esteem. One manager thought they stood above the rest of their staff because of their title. When I'm facilitating a leadership program, I emphasize that titles are cheap (and I always see heads nodding when the penny drops). Your employees are the reason you're in this position. Respect them first and the feelings will be mutual, not the other way around.

- I know another manager who sits behind his desk seven out of eight hours a day typing emails galore, with absolutely no interactive or people skills, and wonders why no one cares about him. He would type the equivalent of a newspaper instead of calling someone and having a personal conversation. Talk about a time waster, or perhaps he just thinks he's too good to speak with customers.

- I happen to know one of the most arrogant service managers who openly told me what he was earning—not sure where he plucked the figure from, but it was huge—and was ignorant enough to say that he must be the highest paid service manager in the country! Really!

- A senior manager once instructed me to tell my staff that if they didn't like the bonus system implemented by the company, they could roll their toolboxes out the door. I was totally shocked and lost all respect for that individual. Clearly, he had no idea how to manage and, again, was only concerned about the bottom line.

Most people I've described here are no longer employed with the same company because of their egos and unprofessional manners. They are just a few of the people without emotional intelligence or with no genuine interest in working with staff, and most definitely no desire to engage or connect with them. Their egos went to their heads. I must also admit that I no longer communicate with them. No prizes for guessing why!

"Changes are hard in the beginning, messy in the middle, but gorgeous in the end."
~ Robin Sharma

Key Notes
Please read *Feel the Fear and Do it Anyway* by Susan Jefferies. The message is that often we fear what we say or do. As a result, we withhold our personal potential from being unleashed. Look deep within, express yourself, and speak the truth. Only then will you be able to be who you want to be and do what you want, without fear. You will thank yourself later and wonder why you never did it years ago.

What is your biggest takeaway from this chapter?

10

Create a Happy Workforce with High Morale

Sociologist Alexander Leighton defines morale as "the capacity of a group of people to pull together persistently and consistently in pursuit of a common purpose."

Management always overlooks morale because we're too focused on the end result, month after month. What most managers fail to understand is that business is about people and processes, and without the engagement of people, you're not going to achieve the result, regardless of the processes you have in place. Morale is hugely beneficial for a thriving organization, so it's essential to develop good morale in your team.

Almost exclusively, organizations with high morale experience higher productivity and staff engagement, show lower employee turnover, and absenteeism, and have a happier workforce. What's more, they find it easier to attract and retain the best talent. While raising morale can seem a nebulous goal, many of its outcomes are measurable, and directly affect the bottom line. Last but not least, it feels great to work in an organization where morale is high!

There are many factors that cause team morale to dip and consequently suffer. For example:
1. Layoffs and restructuring
2. Poor leadership
3. Poor communication
4. Lack of empowerment or autonomy
5. Inflexible working conditions

6. Cancellation of team benefits
7. Damage to the organization's reputation or public image
8. Difficult co-workers
9. Heavy workloads or stress, with no reward or gratitude
10. No sense of social value to the work being done, or work having a negative impact on the wider society
11. Last but not least, a self-centered manager

Signs of Low Morale

Too often, managers don't realize that morale is poor. Whether or not your team or organization is facing one of the above scenarios, watch out for the following clues that morale may be slipping:

- Obvious unhappiness
- Increased complaints about work, or other team members
- Increased absenteeism
- An increase in conflict between team members
- Insubordination or unruliness
- Disorganized work environments
- Increased employee turnover

- Decreased productivity
- Lack of enthusiasm

Leader or Manager Morale

Keep in mind that if you're a leader or manager, your team's morale starts with you. It's up to you to be a good role model for your team. If your own morale is suffering, it's vital you work on rebuilding your outlook and attitude first. Start by identifying why your morale is low, and then come up with ways to adjust your mental attitude.

Often this starts with action. For instance, perhaps your morale is down because your dealer principal is pressuring you to do a good job. Make yourself feel more positive and in control of the situation by getting organized, and by achieving measurable goals that will put your dealer principal at ease.

Work on rebuilding your self-confidence, having self-awareness, and being mindful are things that takes patience and time to work on. Remember that your team is always watching you; if you're feeling positive and confident, they will too. Even the smallest win help builds confidence—for you, and your team.

If your team's morale needs rebuilding, there are several strategies you can use. However, just as you did with your own morale, you need to start by understanding the problem. This helps you choose strategies that best fit your situation, which may include:

- **Reconnect with your team**
  - o Practicing MBWA regularly establish trust and rapport with your team.
- **Develop your team**
  - o Allow every opportunity for your employee to learn.
- **Improve the workplace**
  - o Ensure you are continually improving the workplace. People want to work in a safe and happy environment.
- **Improve communication**
  - o Be honest and transparent at all times to earn trust.
- **Set measurable goals**

o Do this as a team, set your expectations, and ask for their expectation. This is a two-way street for both parties.

- **Build confidence**
  o Empowering your people as well as delegating effectively will bring about confidence and success.
- **Focus on talent management**
  o Implement a succession plan and development program for the future.
- **Keep people motivated**
  o Keep your employees engaged and connected.

Key Notes

Team morale can suffer for many reasons. If you suspect that your team's morale isn't what it should be, you can rebuild it by using the strategies above.

What is your biggest takeaway from this chapter?

11

Facilitate Continuous Improvement

One of the best things you can do as a manager is to implement a continuous improvement plan as part of a great succession plan. Do it right now, even if you have the department ticking like clockwork. Many managers think they don't need one because everything is working smoothly. This is a big mistake. As the name suggests, your processes should be "continuously improving," that is, while everything is above water and nothing is off track, a plan will prevent the opposite from occurring if something does go wrong.

Review all your current processes to see if they will sustain another year. Or, if they can be improved now, don't wait. In a changing workplace environment, there is always a reason to review your continuous improvement plan.

Allow me to share with you my personal continuous improvement plan from when I worked as a manager in the retail business. After 18 years in this position, I decided I needed to do something that could lead me to be a coach, mentor, and facilitator in the industry I had worked in for 30 years. I completed my TAE (Certification in Workplace Training and Assessment) in 2010. The personal continuous improvement plan was my idea, my plan B to be developed in the next stage of my life.

In 2011, I commenced my facilitating role with the view to improving and sharing knowledge as well as establishing a culture of making a difference in other people's lives. I'm very thankful for that opportunity and it opened many doors for me.

Life is like a chess game; you must think one or two steps ahead of your opponent if you want to win. Otherwise you will not be in control of your life. It's important to be in control, in the driver's seat, rather than be reactive and watch what happens. Always have a plan B, not only in your profession, but also in your personal life.

When I started my facilitating and coaching profession, I had long planned to write a self-development book to assist those wanting to be a great service manager, or to be successful in another industry. My aim was always to set people up for success. Throughout my career I have known people who are self-interested and focused only on what they can gain. I have also known genuine people who have assisted me along my path, guiding me to heights than I never could have imagined. I'm truly blessed and grateful to have had those people with me on my journey.

From a personal point of view, I suggest keeping yourself educated and keep learning every day. To give you another example, I knew a person who had worked in a company for about 25 years, doing the same job until one day he was made redundant. Mystified, he questioned the company on his loyalty. The reason was plain and simple: If you don't add value to your position or contribute to the company's success, they don't require you as an employee.

Seize opportunities when they arise. Through self-awareness and training in simple mindfulness techniques, you will achieve self-realization and be able to see opportunities around every corner.

I would like to touch more on the continuous improvement process and why it's so important for all of us to understand that if we don't continue to improve and grow, we are literally going backward.

In the days of your parents and grandparents, customer service was everything. In short, it was very personalized. For instance, a gas attendant would fill your car then check your oil and water; a spare parts person would show you how to fit certain parts and what additional parts may be required; and a doorman was employed to open and close the door for people attending movies, restaurants and hotels—just real old-fashioned customer service. Look at any old movie and you'll see what I'm saying. Unfortunately, an increase in business has made most of us somewhat complacent, but now it seems to have gone full circle and we have returned to providing good old customer service.

Key Notes

One of the mistakes managers make is assuming that work environments or circumstances will remain unchanged, so they take people and processes for granted. Your role is to continue to facilitate and monitor continuous improvement across all the people and processes in your department.

"World-class begins when you think you've done a great job but know you can do a better job." ~ Robin Sharma

What is your biggest takeaway from this chapter?

12

What Your Personal Branding Says About You

This book was written to assist managers look more closely at themselves, gain self-awareness, and see things from a different perspective. We all have personal branding, or an image we project, which affects how others see and think of us. We are all created differently—this defines us. Have a think about what your personal branding is.

Throughout my long, fruitful career in the automotive industry, I had the opportunity to work with some remarkable leaders and exceptional people from all walks of life. They had the traits and habits possessed by all great leaders, and I learned a lot from them. One lesson I'm going to share is the importance of bonding. People are important to leaders and good leaders care what they think.

Leaders take responsibility for their actions and decisions, whether they succeed or make mistakes. Your people are always watching you, listening and judging, just as you're doing to me as you read this book. This is life and, as managers or leaders, we have to live with it. It is imperative to set a good example and be aware of what your intentions are when setting each example.

You need to realize that you're continuously building your reputation, which is what I call personal branding. If you don't live up to this, or if you're not aligned with your words and actions, you will lose credibility and there will be distrust. Sure, not everyone will agree with what you do and how you do it, but "the buck stops with you" (a phrase I learned in Canada). This simply means that when you make a decision, you live with it. I have made mistakes in my career, but in the long term I have learned from those decisions, and so will you.

The reality is that we all judge ourselves by our intentions and decisions, some more harshly than others. People fortunately (or unfortunately) will judge our actions as a result of those decisions. Make the decision that ultimately represents your personal branding. Although we can't undo it, every day is a new day and a new chance to begin again.

Great managers must become coaches to their staff, so set a new course of personal branding that includes the following:

- Choose to understand the challenges faced by your staff
- Choose to create a motivating environment
- Choose to listen with intent and ask questions to get a bigger and better picture
- Choose to be inspirational and assist them with setting goals and standards
- Choose to be positive and grateful (your staff will notice!) and remember that people judge you by your actions

I have also maintained that if you think negatively, you will act negatively. Think positively and you will act positively—that is how nature works.

Not everyone is going to be happy with what you do, but the choices you make today will determine the results or outcomes tomorrow. As the saying goes "What you sow today, you will reap tomorrow."

We all think and react differently, but as long as your intentions are good and fair, you will continue to excel in your personal branding.

Autocratic vs. Democratic Leadership Styles

I personally know some service managers who have completely different work styles, and neither individual get the results they want. Or if they do, the results are not consistent and only short term.

I'm aware of one service manager who has an autocratic style and drives his staff hard, constantly micromanaging to a point where they have zero autonomy to make decisions and learn, simply because they're terrified to make mistakes. Emails and telephone calls come through, continuously requesting authorization. Overall, it's an unpleasant and unproductive environment to work in. His staff turnover is also very high.

The second manager works at the other end of the spectrum with a democratic style. The best way to describe him is a teddy bear who avoids conflict or any confrontation. His staff runs amok in the department and, in order to avoid animosity, he allows them free rein to make decisions; sometimes they repeat their mistakes because he isn't coaching them.

Neither of these service managers should be in their position, and both need to learn about leadership styles. It will be difficult for them to sustain the role long term, and if they do, and they happen to utilize the same styles, the company or organization will suffer. The key is being in the middle of the scale between autocratic and democratic, of course. Unfortunately these managers have large egos that prevent them from admitting that their respective styles don't work, which doesn't help branding.

It's frustrating to know that these leadership styles exist in the workplace today. To strike a balance, the only course of action is to consult a leadership coach. I'm talking from experience here. In my early days, all I wanted to do was impress the stakeholders and my general manager, but I was not doing my staff or myself any favors. I was fortunate to be guided by a performance coach and it was only then that I changed my style to around 60% autocratic and 40% democratic. Needless to say, this changed the mentality and mood of every staff member, as they wanted to be part of my team.

From experience, one thing that can strengthen or weaken your personal branding is organizational alignment. This is a very important factor for success, because if your goals and focus for the future are not aligned with the organization, you're wasting your precious time and effort. Besides that, you will never be happy, and rolling with the punches is no way to enjoy what you're doing.

Organizational alignment is a must if you are to succeed as a manager in any company. I was once employed by a prestigious dealership, and the leadership philosophy of its CEO was the opposite of mine; in fact, not even our thinking was aligned. Having been born and raised in South Africa and learning about styles of management and leadership across the globe, I have developed many important skills. People skills, particularly dealing with people from different cultures, can be extremely difficult and stressful. As we know, customers are not always the reason our roles are challenging at times. Sometimes the hardest part is dealing with staff and their personalities.

A country's culture plays a large part in whether or not a company will succeed in that country, and unfortunately not everyone is on board with that. The CEO had a leadership philosophy that was inflexible when working in different countries. To lead a company and work in a different culture are two different things. Unfortunately, the CEO didn't understand the culture, nor was he prepared to adapt. (Being adaptable and flexible are two traits of great leaders.) After nearly 12 months in the role of service manager, and after reporting to three different dealer principals in that time, all of whom eventually departed, I too decided that the best solution was to leave. I didn't want to waste time stressing about a company that was never going to be successful, no matter what I did. You will be remembered for your branding reputation, so it is paramount to set a good example.

I have been asked what my greatest assets are and what I can bring to assist people or companies. I believe that my talent allows me to see the real person, what lies beneath their exterior, so I'm able to coach them to their full potential. If there is no immediate connection, I can pretty much tell that I won't be able to coach them. This is very different to judging people; it is knowing within yourself that this person doesn't have the talent to move forward. I'm not sure if it's a skill, and sometimes I feel one is born with it—an instinct, or a sixth sense. I do know, however, that my self-awareness makes me different and provides me with an edge.

Key Notes

The above choices are within your power and control. My philosophy on the choices that I live by every day is to make it happen. Your actions are a result of your thoughts and/or intentions. It's up to you to be disciplined and committed to making choices that ensure your personal branding reflects your intentions.

"Even a tiny mosquito leaves a lasting impression." ~ African proverb

What is your biggest takeaway from this chapter?

13
Personal SWOT Analysis

In this chapter, I will discuss how to make the most of your talents and opportunities by utilizing the SWOT analysis on yourself.

SWOT analysis—the acronym stands for strengths, weaknesses, opportunities, and threats—is a useful technique that helps you identify your strengths and weaknesses, and then looks at what opportunities can assist. Think about your strengths and weaknesses in relation to the people around you, and at the same time look for any opportunities to make changes.

Ask yourself the following questions:

Strengths

- What skills/advantages do you have that others don't? For example, certifications, education or contacts.
- What do you do better than anyone else?
- What personal resources can you access?
- What do other people (your manager, in particular) see as your strengths?
- Which of your achievements are you most proud?
- What values do you possess that others fail to exhibit?
- Are you part of a network that no one else is? If so, what connections do you have with influential people?

Weaknesses

- What tasks do you avoid because you don't feel confident doing them?
- What do people around you see as your weaknesses?
- Are you completely confident in your education and skills training? If not, what are your weakest?
- What are your weak work habits? For example, are you often late, are you disorganized, do you have a short temper, or are you poor at handling stress?

Opportunities

- What new technology can help you? Or can you get help from others or via the Internet?
- Is your industry growing? If so, how can you take advantage of the current market?
- Do you have a network of strategic contacts to help you, or offer good advice?
- What trends (management or otherwise) do you see in your company, and how can you take advantage of them?

You might also find useful opportunities in the following:

- Networking events, educational classes, or conferences.
- A colleague going on extended leave. Could you take on some of this person's projects to gain experience?
- A new role or project that forces you to learn new skills, like public speaking.
- A company expansion or acquisition. Do you have specific skills (like a second language) that could help with the process?

Threats

- What obstacles do you currently face at work?
- Are any of your colleagues competing with you for projects or roles?
- Is your job, or the demand for the things you do, changing?
- Does changing technology threaten your position?
- Could any of your weaknesses lead to threats?

Key Notes

The SWOT matrix is a framework for analyzing your strengths and weaknesses as well as potential opportunities and threats you may face. It helps you focus on your strengths, minimize your weaknesses, and takes the greatest possible advantage of opportunities available to you. Be honest when performing this task and set yourself up for success!

What is your biggest takeaway from this chapter?

14
Look the Part

Look the part you want to be. This is crucial. Unfortunately, people judge others on looks, and we all know that first impressions count. There is a saying that "clothes make the man." It might seem like common sense, but you'd be surprised how sloppily some service managers dress, even those who work for prestigious companies. Being well groomed will earn you respect.

There's also that other saying, "You never get a second chance to make a good first impression." Psychologists, writers, and seminar leaders have cautioned that it only takes seven to seventeen seconds of interaction with a stranger before they form an opinion of us. The greatest way to make a positive first impression is to demonstrate immediately that the other person—not you—is the center of the action and conversation.

Years ago, I mentored a service manager from a dealership who was being promoted from within the company. He wore his technician's overalls to the front desk during his role. I explained that he must look the part, as it would distinguish him from the rest of his staff in the workshop and so he decided to change. My view is that if you want to play the right part, you have to wear the right clothes. If you look good and feel good, you will be good at what you do. I once sat next to a person at a conference and commented that she was well dressed. She said, "You have to look the part that you want."

I would like to talk about posture and the way you conduct yourself when managing by walking around. Dressing professionally must follow by behaving professionally. I once worked with a performance coach and he directed me to walk with my shoulders back, not hunched over, and ensure my head was upright and I was looking forwards. Be aware of how you walk and carry yourself; take slow steps and don't rush. You must appear to be in control, even if you're not. When you walk slowly, make eye contact, because it's an opportunity to connect with people.

A few years ago, when I was employed at a dealership as a service manager, I implemented MBWA. I entered the service reception and walked toward the front desk, where a girl was slumped over the keyboard. When she noticed me, she immediately sat upright. I decided to share my theory on how she could improve herself to be the perfect receptionist as the face of the dealership. After a few minutes, I left her with one statement, "If you want to look good, you have to dress well, and you will automatically do and be good." It didn't take her long to look the part of a professional receptionist and, as a result, her posture and work skills also improved.

When greeting or thanking customers or staff, always be first to shake hands. Extending your hand first is a sign of peace, be mindful of different cultures..

Appearance counts. True, standards for appropriate attire have changed drastically over the years, but it's still very important. Maybe the best advice I can share came from a participant I met at a seminar. She said, "Tony, I don't dress for the job I have now, I dress for the job I want to have." In my time, I've actually worked with a few service managers that looked the part but had no idea of the role. Looking the part can make a huge difference.

I must point out that an individual's speaking style also impacts a first impression, maybe more than we think. Listeners judge our intelligence, our cultural level, our education and even our leadership ability by the words we select and how we speak to them.

Key Notes

When making a positive first impression, always remember to demonstrate immediately that the other person—not you—is the centre of the conversation. Dress appropriately for the occasion, especially if there's a position you have your sights on. Learn to listen and acknowledge; this is a sure way to build rapport. And remember: First impressions always count.

What is your biggest takeaway from this chapter?

15
Attitude

Attitude is 10% of what has happened and 90% how you deal with it. This can make or break you on any given day, and can lead to positive or negative results depending on your reaction to the circumstances. To succeed in your position, attitude counts for 50%. Get that right and you're halfway there. The same can be said for staff members you're coaching and training. The right attitude means being positive and being in the right frame of mind. This will lead to profits in the long term.

Attitude means that you understand yourself, and you know that the only person who can change is you. This is called self-awareness—a combination of your internal attention and your focus. The most important person in this universe is you, so learn to understand and know yourself. Without self-awareness, you will continue to make the same mistakes. This will lead to disarray in your processes, your results, and your decisions long term. I made many mistakes in my early years; I had a bad attitude and there was no one to make me aware of it.

When I was facilitating, I used the three P's: thinking positive, acting positive, and being positive. Some smart people caught onto this and understood that it was all about attitude. Positive thoughts lead to a positive attitude; it's a simple formula.

Positive Attitude and Outlook

A positive mindset is also associated with strong leadership. However, being positive is much more than presenting a happy face to the world. You also need to develop a strong sense of balance and recognize that setbacks and problems will occur. What makes the difference is how you deal with them.

Positive people approach situations realistically; they're prepared to make the changes necessary to overcome a problem. Negative people, on the other hand, often give in to the stress and pressure of a situation. This can lead to fear, worry, distress, anger, and failure as well as actions they later will regret. Attitude means everything to your success in this role. Concentrate on the fundamentals, because 99% of all success is achieved this way.

As a manager of a department, whatever attitude you bring to the table is the attitude your staff will take with them when they leave. It starts with you and ends with you.

Perception is reality—what people see and think is what they believe, even if that isn't the whole truth. In my coaching courses, I often talk about first impressions and perceptions, because it's rare to get a second chance to make a great first impression. You often only have one chance and that's it.

Key Notes
I will end with a little thought: If you always think positively, you will act with positive intentions, and as a result everything will be positive.

"We can complain because rose bushes have thorns, or rejoice because thorn bushes have roses."
~ Abraham Lincoln

What is your biggest takeaway from this chapter?

16
Delegate Effectively

Who delegates and who doesn't is the difference between succeeding and not succeeding. Delegation is an area of personal and professional management that many people struggle with. Rather than working on improving our delegation skills, the mistake we make is keeping hold of more tasks and, before we know it, we're burned out. Learning the skill of delegation should be a top priority for service managers or those in similar positions.

The Importance of Delegation

Delegation should be a top priority for managers no matter how skilled you are. There's only so much you can achieve working on your own. With a team, you can achieve so much more, and this is more reason to delegate effectively.

The key to my success is the little secret of delegating effectively. I use the word secret because many people have no idea how to delegate and wonder why it takes them twice as long to achieve the results they want. Delegation means taking true responsibility, inevitably giving up some control and learning to let it go. Don't be a control freak. Besides, you can't be everywhere, and if mistakes are made, that's a way for everyone to learn.

I once went to a conference with my wife in the United States and decided to organize a huge vacation around it. The one-week conference was in Las Vegas. Afterward, we headed off to Toronto to see my siblings for a week and to Montreal for a few days. We visited Disneyland in Florida for another week and went to Los Angeles before heading back to Australia. The total time spent, including a stopover for a few days in Singapore, was five weeks. When I returned to work after this period, I was shocked. Why? Well, my desk was clean and there were literally no papers in my in folder. I thought I was fired. This, my friends, is because of effective and successful delegation. I could have spent another five weeks overseas. I have been asked on a few occasions at meetings and seminars why my phone doesn't ring, and why I always seem to have time on my hands. The secret is simple: I delegate effectively. You can't do everything on your own. I used to joke with a straight face that the more others do for me, the less I have to do and the more time I can spend on the golf course working on my game. On the other hand, there's truth in that statement, because it allows me more time to plan and work on the business.

Personally, I think 30% of our time should be thinking or planning, 30% doing what you require in your role, and 30% engaging with your people. If you can relate to that formula and balance, you will no doubt be successful and in perfect harmony. This is why delegation is such an important skill, and one that you absolutely have to learn. Successful people delegate. That's it.

How You Should Delegate

Use the following principles to delegate successfully:

1. Envision what the end result looks like when you want to delegate a task.

2. Communication is paramount and transparency around clarity for both persons is key when the following are considered:

   - Waiting to be told what to do.

   - Asking what to do.

   - Recommending what should be done, and then act on it.

   - Initiating action and then reporting on it periodically.

3. Discuss with your employees when and what tasks are to be delegated to them.

4. Ensure that your employees are responsible for the tasks, allowing them to make

    decisions while reiterating that you're supporting them.

5. Set people up for success and delegate using your discretion; that is, give them tasks that stretch within their ability.

6. Feedback periodically is crucial for their development.

7. Empowering your employees to always find the most effective and efficient methods to perform their tasks. Exercise autonomy.

8. Celebrate success if the goals are reached; this builds confidence and trust. You will be surprised what they can and will do for you.

Some delegation tips:

- Realize that you just can't do it all; everyone has limits.

- Start delegating small easy tasks, one step at a time

- Delegation is a skill that takes patience, persistence, and practice.

- Recognize and celebrate success together when a task is completed.

- Be prepared to accept feedback from your employees as well; this is a learning journey for them and they could have another method to reach the same goal

- Supporting your employees through their tasks is important
- The more tasks you delegate, the more time you will have to do other important tasks.
- Part of succession planning is getting the right people to do the right tasks.

Successful delegation starts with matching people and tasks, so you first need to explain what your team's role and goal is. Defining their work roles is important and what your expectations for them are. It is best practice to think about your backup plan in the event that the other person isn't available. That way there's no missing or weak link in the chain. I would suggest always training two persons for the same tasks and how you can achieve this would be to alternate a task between two people. It is imperative that you spend time on this skill. Mastering it will enable you to do the 30/30/30 formula as previously explained.

Delegation, done well, benefits everyone. Your employees have more opportunities to expand and enrich their roles through empowerment and they will have learned a new skill. So, if you're not delegating, you're moving backward, and you can't afford to. You will be even better in your role and, with a little courage to "let go," you'll be amazed by what you and your team can achieve.

Key Notes

One key piece of advice I can offer is to "let go." If you're not letting go and delegating, you won't move forward and progress with your career. Once again: You can't do it all and if you want to succeed, you must delegate wisely and follow through to ensure that the process is followed. It's that simple!

What is your biggest takeaway from this chapter?

17
Trust

Google's dictionary defines trust as the "firm belief in the reliability, truth, or ability of someone or something."

Why does trust matter as a manager? Trust is a huge attribute of great leadership, and you can't build trust with others if you don't first trust yourself. If you want to develop as a good leader, you must first understand how to regain self-trust (if it has been lost). Let me ask you this: Have you ever made a commitment to yourself and not followed through? Whether it's business, health or finance, we've all done it.

There are two things you must understand about developing trust. The first is to know the people you're working with. If you're spending 70% to 80% of your time with the same people on a daily basis (that's approximately 1,400 hours a year), you must work and develop together, trusting each other with respective tasks as a team. The second thing to understand about developing mutual trust is earning that trust. When I'm facilitating, I constantly communicate and follow up with my audience, sending them reminder emails for sessions they were attending and checking if they required assistance with assignments or pre-work. I wanted them to feel comfortable and to develop trust between us.

If I've asked five different people what enables them to trust another person, I would get at least three different answers, usually relating to honesty and reliability. Over the years there are a few that stick in my mind that I will share with you.

Integrity and respect are on top of my list. This has been instilled since my strict discipline childhood upbringing. Being available and making time for your people is important in order for them to come to you at any time. Being fair when evaluating situations or treating everyone equally is paramount. I can honestly say that at times I may be hard on certain situations and employees, but I've always treated everyone fairly. Empowering your people to make decisions will earn you trust, which in turn allows them to learn and progress in their career. My last item is transparency. Effective communication and being open with your people is another way to gain trust and respect.

Apprenticeship and Trust

When I was facilitating apprenticeship groups, I treated them with the same respect as anyone else. They would confide in me and seek my advice purely because they felt comfortable with our level of trust. Respectfully, the problem with some managers is that they don't have defined values. It's all about what they can gain today and, as a result, trust flies out the window (and it's very difficult to earn back). I compare trust to a mirror: Once it is broken or cracked, you can never fully mend it.

I have been criticized in the past about how I handled situations with apprentices who made mistakes. It's often easier to criticize people than to praise them and see the good in them. Service managers can even inadvertently dissuade the younger generation to take up apprenticeships if they are treated harshly. They tend to forget that they themselves were given opportunities to learn as an apprentice, technician or service advisor prior to their present position, and perhaps they even made the same mistakes, or worse.

Key Notes

People will only respect you once they trust you, and that is my top priority when it comes to being a great leader. Trust in your people and they will trust you.

What is your biggest takeaway from this chapter?

18
People vs. Process

Yes, you need both people and processes in business to survive, and one can't exist without the other. They are your greatest assets. We knew this many years ago, but to be highly successful and sustainable in the industry today and to move forward, you need the right people and the right processes to be perfectly balanced.

Part of your department succession planning should include this theory. If performance isn't up to par, or if the process no longer applies, have the courage to change it while you have the opportunity, now rather than later. The longer you wait to make changes, the worse off your department will be long term.

Processes are important in every business to regulate desired outcomes. They form risk management, and any abnormalities that could occur, will occur, if they aren't in place. Forget processes introduced five or ten years ago; they are probably outdated and don't apply now. Also, chances are good they were never reviewed because a contingency plan or continuous improvement plan was never introduced in the first place. Many companies implement a process and think of it is a means to an end without reviewing it again for years. No one has a crystal ball to see if it will work in the future. But look at how the world has changed in just the last decade, and how manufacturers have changed their guidelines accordingly to meet the global standards.

Your processes must be part of your continuous improvement plan, to be reviewed on an annual basis. Here's a question to ask yourself and your team: Is this process operational to optimize customer satisfaction and profitability or/and is there a better way to improve this process? Have a continuous improvement plan and always endeavor to improve what you did today, to make a point of difference tomorrow.

If you can get the right people and the right processes to combine seamlessly, you will have a winning combination. This formula equates to monumental profitability. The same philosophy applies to the sales, parts, and any other department.

One afternoon, a dealer principal from another franchise rang me and was livid about the internal mystery caller results he had received. His words were, "We have a real problem ... should have done this years ago ... might not be in this position today, especially under the present climate of the economy and definitely can't afford the bad, unprofessional service we give on the phone." Hindsight is a wonderful thing, and this Chinese proverb says it best: "The best time to plant a tree was twenty years ago, the second best time is yesterday."

Right, imagine that same situation if you had the wrong people running the department for many years. How much profit and how many opportunities would you have missed? Instead of recovering your costs in five years, it would take you ten years or longer because you had the incorrect people operating the business, the incorrect processes that were no longer relevant, and no continuous improvement plan in place.

One bad habit is complacency, and that explains the above scenario. With no proper training, coaching, or mentoring, a manager will not be effective. They will also develop bad habits that will eventually flow down to their staff. Before you know it, the whole department is just going through the motions, turning up every day and collecting an income with the what's in it for me mentality. They were probably the right people when they were recruited, but bad habits slipped through the cracks as a result of bad management. It doesn't take long before a process becomes a total waste of time with no or minimal benefit, because no one is working from the same page.

How to Keep Your Department on Top of Their Game

1. **Mystery shoppers in the dealership.** This ensures that everyone is on the same page and focused on getting the car fixed properly the first time, as per manufacturer expertise. Remember, first impressions are everything in life. Getting the business and selling the benefit of your dealership is what will keep your department profitable.

2. **Team-bonding exercises**. Have a meeting outside your work premises in a completely different environment. Have a team-building session involving everyone from every department. The more they understand each other, the more they will want to work with each other.

3. **Innovative and creative people who think outside the box.** For example, why would you provide a loan car to a customer who has the same model? Provide the upgraded model if their mileage is high. You must start coaching your staff to think outside the box.

4. **Have reports queued to your email every morning or week.** These should mainly focus on profitability. For example, a no-charge invoice to please explain why, or an open work-in-progress report, or even a simple scenario such as no email details on a work order report.

Trust your people to work as efficiently and professionally as they can, coaching them at all possible times, because if they're good at what they do, you will have the respect you deserve and subsequently you'll have your own peace of mind.

Key Notes
Continue to improve the touch points of what you and your staff do every day. Have weekly meetings

to facilitate this as part of the process going forward.

People:

- Take your time recruiting the right people for the right role
- Swiftly dismiss what doesn't work, as in "don't carry any passengers"
- Ensure there are always clear expectations and mutual understanding
- Be committed to and supportive of your employees

Process (must be derived from):

- Your mission and vision statement
- What your company and organizational policies stand for
- Expressing clarity from both sides when implementing a process
- Consistency in your approach when addressing a process
- Certain processes are non-negotiable and must be adhered to

What is your biggest takeaway from this chapter?

19
Common Leadership and Management Mistakes

It's often said that mistakes provide great learning opportunities. However, it's much better not to make mistakes in the first place! We're looking at the most common leadership and management errors, and highlighting what you can do to avoid them. If you can learn about them here, rather than through experience, you'll save yourself a lot of trouble.

1. Lack of feedback

Failing to provide feedback to your people is the most common mistake leaders make. When you don't provide prompt feedback, you're depriving them of the opportunity to improve their performance. Feedback is the breakfast of champions.

It's a tool to master, for it's the only way you and your people can grow and be more effective. It's also one of the best tools to maximize production and enhance your leadership skills. In saying that, asking for feedback is equally important in order for you to grow and advance personally.

2. Not making time for your team

When you're a manager or leader, it's easy to get so wrapped up in your workload that you don't make yourself available to your team. Your people must always come first. When you're not available when you're needed, they won't know what to do, and they won't have the support and guidance they need to meet their objectives, which can be a recipe for failure. Avoid this mistake by blocking out time in your schedule and learning how to listen actively to your team. Adapt a "door is always open" policy and practice MBWA as outlined in other chapters. Remember, you're only as good as your people.

3. Being too "hands-off"

Example: One of your team members has just completed an important project. The problem is that he misunderstood the project's specification, and you didn't stay in touch with him as he worked on it. Now, he's completed the project and repairs the wrong way, and you're faced with explaining this to an angry client, and even worse, failing to meet their expectations. Avoid micromanagement at all costs, but stay in touch and be aware of what your people are doing on a daily or weekly basis. Always be there for your people; hence the importance of meetings!

4. Being too friendly

Most of us want to be friendly to people in our team. After all, people are happier when they get on with their manager. However, you'll sometimes have to make tough decisions to get the balance right between friendliness and authority. Make sure that you set clear boundaries so that team members aren't tempted to take advantage of you.

5. Failing to define goals or set expectations

When your people don't have clear goals, they muddle through their day. They can't be productive if they have no idea what they're working towards. That is one of my formulas for success: *Clarity* (from Tony's three C's). Avoid this mistake by learning to set smart goals for your team. Also realize that both parties have expectations, so meet to discuss these goals often.

6. Misunderstanding motivation

Do you know what truly motivates your team? Chances are good that it's not just money! Many leaders make the mistake of thinking their team is only working for monetary rewards. For example, people seeking a greater work-life balance might be motivated by flexible working hours. Others will be motivated by factors such as achievement, training, extra responsibility, praise, or a sense of camaraderie.

7. Hurrying recruitment

It's important to have a full team, but filling a vacant role too quickly to make up numbers can be disastrous. Hurrying recruitment can lead to recruiting the wrong people for your team. Remember, always hire for attitude—the number one rule—and be particularly picky about the people you bring in. They have to adapt and fit into your team, not vice versa.

8. Not "walking the walk"

If you make personal telephone calls during work time, or speak negatively about your CEO, you can expect your team to do this too. As a leader, you need to be a role model for your team. This means that if they need to stay late, you should also stay late to help them. Or, if your organization has a rule that no one eats at their desk, then set the example and head to the lunch room every day for lunch. The same goes for your attitude: If you're negative some of the time, you can't expect your people not to be negative. Remember that your team is always watching. If you want to shape their behavior, start with your own. They'll follow suit.

9. Not delegating

Some managers don't delegate because they feel that no one apart from them can do key jobs properly. This can cause huge problems—work bottlenecks around them and they become stressed and burned out. Unless you delegate tasks, you're never going to have time to focus on the broader work responsibilities of most leaders and managers. What's more, you'll fail to develop your people to take the pressure off you and won't develop a trusting relationship.

10. Misunderstanding your role

Once you become a leader or manager, your responsibilities are very different from those you had before. However, it's easy to forget that your job has changed, and that you should now use a different set of skills to be effective. This results in you not doing what you've been hired to do: to lead and to manage. While you were hired to be a manager, you role should be more focused on being a leader and coach moving forward.

Key Notes

We all make mistakes, even leaders and managers, who sometimes fail to give constructive feedback, are too "hands-off," and don't delegate effectively or misunderstand your role. It's true that making a mistake can be a learning opportunity, but taking the time to recognize and avoid common mistakes can help you become productive and successful—and highly respected by your team.

What is your biggest takeaway from this chapter?

20
The "What Would Tony Foon Do" Strategy

I have always maintained the following philosophy: "If I'm going to be the best at what I do, I must first and foremost understand everything that I need to know." The first part of this philosophy is that I need to understand, so *clarity* is very important, hence the first C in my three C's is exactly that. The second part of my strategy is that I must be disciplined, and therefore the next C is *commitment*. The third part of my strategy is that I must follow a pattern that works for me and is also successful, therefore the last C is *consistency*—everything that I am and do is what I stand for, always. To sum up, I'm talking about expectations, both yours and those of your staff. If you're clear, committed, and consistent in what you do, your staff will be too.

As I mentioned earlier, you should continually ask your staff the right questions and thereby empower your employees. This draws together two characteristics of leadership. The first is that they are accountable and the second is that you're allowing them to think outside the box.

Let's look at accountability. You're asking people to think about the options and to decide what to do, which makes them accountable for their decisions. This says that you respect and trust them. Allowing them to think outside the box, even if they make a mistake, it's also about respect and trust. Everybody learns from mistakes—not your mistakes, but their mistakes.

In my lectures, I often state that I pray for the strength to endure a hard life, meaning that if I make a mistake, I want to have the strength and the ability to recognize it, rectify it and move on. I'm sharing with you what worked for me, so you don't walk down the same road and make the same mistakes. In saying that, you might find a better way to deal with the same scenario, and I truly hope you do. We're all different people who think differently and therefore behave differently. The point is that you have to develop your own style and decide what works for you in the long term.

In my previous role as service manager of one of the largest dealerships in the Southern Hemisphere, I had seven service advisors reporting to me, together with a receptionist, an assistant service manager, two full time drivers and a costing clerk— that was just the frontline staff. In the workshop, I had a workshop manager, four team leaders, and about 40 technicians and apprentices I was accountable for. Coaching a total of about 65 staff isn't an easy task for a service manager. I had to think of a strategy that would benefit everyone, including me. My strategy was the three C's. However, there's another acronym I used that was very effective: What Would Tony Foon Do (WWTFD), which simply required them to think outside the box and come to me with solutions rather than questions, as I wasn't there to perform their role. I actually used a labeling machine and printed the acronym WWTFD and stuck it on top of their monitor screens. Once they adopted this strategy, it worked like a charm, because all of a sudden they had been asked to extend their thinking further.

Coaching and development encourages people to welcome learning opportunities, especially for generations just arriving in the workforce. Telling them what to do almost certainly doesn't work. It's all about why they do it and how they do it, so they can reap the fulfillment of the role. Only then will they be effective moving forward.

This helps with autonomy and empowerment. Educating staff to run the business like their own is possibly the best lesson you can offer. Let them make decisions, give them some ownership, and see how everything flows—and when it doesn't, they will figure it out. The best thing you can do for your employees is to allow them to own a problem and solve it.

Key Notes

I would like to share a few things that made me amazing in the eyes of my employees:

- I empowered my staff to think outside the box and risk making mistakes. The only reason I am where I am is because I have made mistakes in the past.
- I coached my employees to be creative thinkers—a natural process that let them express their ideas.
- I created a welcoming environment, which made them love coming to work. The old saying, "sharing is caring," rings very true. If you care, they will care.
- I trained, coached, and mentored; this is the role of future leaders. If you're not doing these things, now is the time to start.
- I held compulsory meetings to motivate the staff. How else do you communicate and

encourage people to feel excited about themselves?

- I generated a happy atmosphere in the workplace. They spend the most time with you, so it's important to maintain positivity.
- I set expectations and role accountability.
- I utilized praise and gratitude; these help staff with the confidence to achieve their goals.

What is your biggest takeaway from this chapter?

21
Human Resources

HR departments can either be helpful or be a hindrance, depending on the company and the department's intentions. Some HR departments work for the employee first and the company second, and others will stand behind the success of the company and put you second. In the past, I have worked for really fantastic people who handled situations with empathy and professionalism. However, I've also worked for some obnoxious and ignorant people. Use your discretion to determine their agenda and, once you know it, play their game and use it to your advantage.

In one instance I did the opposite—I tried to do the right thing by the company—but unfortunately the HR department had the final verdict on everything. At times, they would not give me the benefit of the doubt, which made my life difficult. To make matters worse, I had an ego at that particular time too which exacerbated the situation, and consequently I learned the hard way. Always use common sense and discretion when making a decision, whether it turns out to be right or wrong.

I have also since learned that no matter your intentions, always document awkward situations, as you never know when you'll need to refer back to them. You will never remember all of the events, facts, and data.

Another example comes to mind I would like to share with you. Back in early 2008, an employee was road testing a sports model on Kings Way in South Melbourne—a very busy road with a speed limit of between 50 and 60 kms. A policeman in a cruiser who was driving in the opposite direction witnessed him going at a very high speed. When the policeman called me, his words were: "He was definitely not going at 60 kms, I can assure you ... I was on the opposite side of the road and saw him driving with a trade plate, so I presume it's a new car that's not registered." There were tram tracks and barriers between the two sides of the road, so crossing over was very difficult, hence the call from the officer. He asked me to please warn the employee that he wasn't only endangering his own life but the lives of others. Later that day, I ascertained who the technician was and asked him to explain why he was going at a high speed and endangering the public. He denied any wrongdoing and didn't take any responsibility. He then reported the conversation to HR, accusing me of harassing and bullying him, and furthermore concocting a story to scare him.

In hindsight, I should have obtained the officer's name and badge number so that I could back up my story, or better still, asked HR to talk to him with all the evidence in hand. You can never be too careful who you're dealing with when it comes to employees. I've always said that managing difficult customers is the easy part. It's managing employees that is the most challenging part of your role as a manager.

Being proactive is a great skill. Some learn it at an early stage; some learn it from making silly mistakes during their career. Either way, start developing the skill of being proactive in everything that you do. "The early bird catches the worm," as the saying goes. Don't wait for something to happen; be prepared to make it happen. Ensure that you document important events, situations and/or circumstances, because sometimes you'll need to refer to them—like the employee that broke the rules and got away with it.

Recruiting the Best People

Ensuring that you employ the best possible people for your organization is one of the keys to successful recruiting. Companies must develop high standards for recruiting, interviewing, selecting, inducting, training, delegating as well as engaging in mentoring and career counseling. The inability to retain good employees beyond the short term is a serious management problem for many companies. Employees who are often unsatisfied in their jobs and can't see a future career with their employers will leave.

A company that wants to offer excellent service needs to employ the right people to perform the service or tasks. A saying that has stuck with me all through these years is "hire slowly and fire fast." Simply take your time to hire the right person with the right attitude.

Employment Checklist

Service Manager as Human Resources

A service department is only as good as its people. Therefore, investing in the right people means investing in service quality. Companies that realize this will:

- Compete aggressively for talent market share
- Offer purpose and meaning to the workplace that people want
- Build employees' skills so they perform their roles competently

- Bring staff together to enjoy the benefits as a team.
- Nurture achievement through measurement and rewards
- Encourage empowerment and learning
- Allow employees' the autonomy and freedom to make decisions

These seven questions are precursors to an action checklist that all managers should be aware of:

1. Are we looking for the right and the best people for our company, or do we just simply fill vacancies?
2. What is the culture like, and would people want to work in our workplace? Is it different to other cultures?
3. Are we visiting in training as a priority to ensure our people are competent in their role?
4. Have we got a team environment culture, and do we work as a team with everybody getting along with each other?
5. Do we allow our employees the autonomy to make decisions in the interest of customer satisfaction?

6. Are we motivating, praising, and rewarding our people to do well, and more important, do we recognize them for the efforts accordingly?
7. Do we listen to everybody in the dealership including the receptionist and the barrister to get ideas to succeed?

Role Clarity

Role clarity has a big impact on organizational success. Uncertainty about what should be done, and how, can dramatically affect both individual and organizational performance. Employees need to focus on having a clear understanding of the roles and responsibilities required for their positions, and for the positions of their team members. Organizations that have high employee engagement have employees that know, understand, and execute their roles and responsibilities. Role clarification is a significant element for gaining organizational success. It's one of the management essentials that make a difference to organizational performance. This is paramount for you as a manager to sit with the newly recruit employee to go through the position description. Whatever the cause, efforts must be made to clarify the required changes in duties and responsibilities.

Key Notes

Hire for character and train for competence; you can't train character. Just like tree roots, it is character that determines you as a person; it is unchangeable. However, you can reposition the branches to grow straight, if required. If the employee you recruit or assign expectations to isn't aligned with you or the organization, cut your losses and move on before it's too late. Damage done earlier is easier to rectify than damage done later, if that makes sense.

Please Note:

Due to ever-changing industrial laws and best practices, my advice would be to consult the HR department prior to making any final decisions on any circumstance or situation. The above examples were written based on my personal past experiences.

What is your biggest takeaway from this chapter?

22
Manage Conflict Priorities

Dealing with Unhappy Customers and Employees

Many of us have to deal with angry or unhappy clients as part of our roles, and it's never easy. But if we know what to say and, more important, how to say it, we may be able to save the situation. In fact, we can even end up with a better relationship with our client than we had before. This is your chance to turn a challenge into an opportunity. Below are specific tips and techniques that you can use to smooth things over and leave them feeling satisfied.

Step One: Adjust Your Mindset

Once you're aware that a client is unhappy, the first thing to do is put yourself into a customer service mindset, or imagine what it feels like to walk in their shoes. What matters is that you realize your customer or client is upset, and that it's up to you to solve the problem. Adjust your mindset so you're giving 100% of your focus to the client, and to the current situation.

Step Two: Listen Actively

The most important step in this process is to listen attentively to what your customer is saying. They want to be heard, so let them air their grievances. Start the dialogue with a neutral statement, such as, "Would you mind if we could go over what happened," or "Please tell me why you're upset." This creates a partnership between you and your client, and it lets them know you're ready to listen and respect them as a customer. Time and time again, I've seen managers focus on justifying their own position. Frankly, this is short-term thinking and, in my opinion, who cares? Just fix the customer's problem. Your ego must be put aside because it doesn't pay the bills. Also, don't allow anything to interrupt this conversation. Give your client all of your attention.

Step Three: Repeat Their Concerns

Once the customer has had time to explain why they're upset, ask questions to make sure you've identified the problem correctly. Use calm, objective wording, as you do not want a confrontation. Repeating the problem shows the customer you were listening, which can help lower their anger and stress level. More than this, it helps you both to clarify the problem that needs solving. You could also use a technique called the spider diagram, which demonstrates that you have been listening by summarizing and repeating their concerns.

Step Four: Be Empathic and Apologize

Once you understand your client's concerns, be empathetic to the situation. Show them you understand why they're upset and make sure your body language communicates this. For example, you could say, "I'm very sorry that we didn't get the car to you on time, especially since the delay has caused these problems," then fix it.

Step Five: Present a Solution

Now you need to present them with a solution. There are two ways to do this. If you feel you know what will make your client happy, tell them how you'd like to correct the situation. If you're not sure you know what your client wants, or if they resist your proposed solution, give them the power to resolve things. Ask them to identify what will make them happy. For instance, you could say, "If that solution doesn't work for you, I'd love to hear what will make you happy. If it's within my power, I'll get it done, and if it's not possible, we can work on another solution together." I once asked an irate customer why he was so hostile and what I did personally to upset him. He didn't explain, but he did apologize for his behavior. Remember, it's never, ever personal. People get caught up in their emotions and say things they later regret.

Step Six: Take Action and Follow Up

Once you've both agreed on a solution, you need to take action immediately. Explain every step you're going to take to fix the problem. Once the situation has been resolved, follow up with your client over the next few days to make sure they are happy. Whenever you can, exceed their expectations. For instance, you could send them a gift certificate, give them a discount on their next purchase, a bottle of wine, flowers or chocolates, or send a hand-written apology.

Step Seven: Use the Feedback

Your last step is to reduce the risk of the situation happening again. If you haven't already, identify how the problem started. Was the wrong part ordered in? Did a service booking receptionist forget to confirm a mobility transport with you? Find the root cause of the problem and make sure it's fixed immediately. Then consider using "Kaizen," a Japanese word that means "change for the better." This is an ideal approach to adopt in order to create continuous improvement in your workplace. Also, ensure that you're managing complaints and feedback effectively.

Further Tips

- It's important to handle difficult customers professionally. If you feel that your client is being unreasonable, you might start to get upset, especially if they're criticizing you or your organization unfairly. Learning to remain calm under pressure can help you get through challenging situations with grace and professionalism.

- If your client is especially angry, then talk slowly and calmly, using a normal tone of voice. This will subtly help lower the tension and ensure that you don't escalate the situation by visibly getting stressed or upset yourself. Meditation over the years has assisted me in this department.

- If your client has sent you a difficult email, or they're angry with you over the phone, then offer to meet with them in person to address the problem. This will not only diffuse anger (it's difficult for most people to get truly angry face to face), but it also shows that you genuinely want to address and fix the situation. I always use this technique when it's a difficult situation.

- Occasionally a client or customer may become verbally abusive toward you or your staff. Prepare in advance what you'll tolerate, and what you won't. If things escalate, you may need to be assertive and stand up for yourself, or even walk away from the situation to give the client time to cool down. There were occasions where I had to ask the customer to leave the premises.

- People in your team might be the ones on the frontline when it comes to difficult customers. Make sure they know how to be managing their own emotions when dealing with difficult people.

Conflict in the Workplace

In many cases, conflict in the workplace is a fact of life; it is inevitable. We're dealing with different personalities, different cultures and different wants and needs, so it's no surprise that we all have a difference of opinion.

The fact that conflict exists, however, isn't necessarily a bad thing. If it's resolved effectively, it can lead to personal and professional growth, and make the difference between positive and negative outcomes.

The good news is that resolving workplace conflict successfully indicates team cohesion, which promotes stronger mutual respect and a renewed faith in the team's ability to work together.

However, if workplace conflict isn't handled effectively, the results can be damaging. Be aware of different personalities that might cause the team to fragment, as this will cause people to become disengaged from their work, which may end in a downward spiral of negativity and low morale.

Every situation is different, regardless of circumstances or how you choose to react. Learn to adapt with a style that works for you. Once you start implementing different strategies and different approaches for outcomes, you will get a feel for what works. Because we're dealing with human personalities and feelings, this can be a subjective process. It's the same for the employees you're managing or customer issues you're resolving. Finding the balance is key to mastering how to react, because behind every action there's a reaction.

Key Notes

- Dealing with difficult customers or employees can be challenging, but if you handle the situation well, you may be able to improve your relationship.
- Ask questions to get clarity until you understand the issue
- Make sure you listen actively to their problems or complaints
- Allow them to vent and don't interrupt or solve the problem right away.
- Be empathic and understanding, and make sure your body language matches this.
- If you don't know how to fix the situation, then ask your client what will make them happy.
- Follow up with your customer to make sure they are satisfied with the resolution.

What is your biggest takeaway from this chapter?

23
The Physicality of a Service Manager

Many of us are very familiar with the physicality of our role. Being tired at the end of the day and looking forward to just shutting our eyes to the outside world is something we all look forward each day. At times you get so drained from the outside influences that you often wonder how you even made it through the day. Many of my colleagues' resort to a glass of wine or two, just to be able to unwind and finally relax.

The stress of our position can take it out on even the most resilient person like me. For most of us, our minds can become cluttered with a multitude of issues, trapping us in problems or challenges on a daily basis. To master ourselves, and escape this mental, emotional, and physical state, we need to learn how to be able to think clearly and be in the moment, otherwise we just end up creating the old lifestyle we're trying to escape. You have to try to find out what works for you to give you that peace of mind. Many years ago, I initiated a relaxing routine that I try to do every day. I begin my day with meditation, then yoga, then Tai chi, a slow form of martial arts, and then culminating in some time that's set aside for reading. Any technology-related work is something I try to do last.

Even technology can be a double-edged sword. Access to email, Skype, Zoom, and smart phones have made our lives easier in some respects. We can now access the Internet from many platforms, giving us the capacity to work from home and, in theory, achieve a better work-life balance. But has this indirectly increased the hours we work?

I now want to share with you four main strategies that have helped me to achieve a better work-life balance, and it is my hope that if implemented, these same strategies will give you similar results and benefits, assisting you in work to live rather than live to work.

Work smarter, not harder

The first one in our lineup is to work smarter rather than harder. We all know that there are certain things we can't control in life: the overzealous boss, people's attitude and behaviors, the crazy weather (especially if you live in Melbourne, Australia), and the occasional traffic. It's not what happen to us in life that matter as much but rather how we react to it. Instead of adding more hours to your workload, learn how to develop systems, processes, and strategies to maximize your time. Discover if there are ways to do whatever tasks effectively and efficiently. Test and try an idea. Assess it to see if it made a difference. There are many insights, tips, and references on how to do this in my book.

Set boundaries

Another useful strategy I've used during the years is to set boundaries. This can be as simple as turning off your mobile phone or avoid checking work emails after your workday has ended. By setting boundaries about your works hours, you push yourself unconsciously to make better use of the hours you have available during the day. In doing so you're creating a healthier and happier lifestyle, which is the objective.

Make your health a top priority

The third strategy I used often is to look after my health. If you have ever been in a demanding position, you know very well how the workload and stress can take a toll on your life and health. Your health should not be something you compromise. Take time to relax, unwind, rest and sleep. You will feel recharged, energized and even able to take on more tasks. Think of work and your career as a pleasurable marathon where you have the luck to experience beautiful learning adventures, awesome achievements, and to learn more about life, yourself and others, rather than as a sprint that leaves you exhausted and frustrated. If you refer to my future chapters it will provide you with knowledge of how I managed to find time for my health and well-being. Remember, there's only one of you.

Get a life!

The last strategy in this chapter I want to share is this: Use your job as the foundation and the financial support for what you love doing. We spend twenty years of our lives finding our place in the world, another thirty years to refine our expertise and skills, and the rest to enjoy our lives. Many may fall into a routine of working extra hours because they simply don't have other things to do outside of work. However, this doesn't have to be the way. If we look at our work as a way to finance our lives, dreams, and aspirations, then we would need to wait to live, if that makes sense. We can live now and find something we are passionate about and use our roles as the foundation for what we love doing, our hobbies, and talents.

Follow this advice and you will be happily on your way to tipping the scales in favor of a work-life balance. Finding time for work, life, and play is very important. If it's a constant challenge to find a workable balance among the three, you may want to think about changing your role, finding a job in a different location, or even changing careers to help achieve it. I get up at 5 A.M. every single morning with the occasional sleep-in till 6 A.M. on weekends. I meditate for an hour and then stretch with yoga before turning to Tai chi for about forty minutes. I walk as often as I possibly can and, and when time permits, I play a round of golf.

I wish I had started meditating earlier in my life. Who knows? I might have been a better manager than I was. In saying that, I have no regrets. I highly recommend looking into it. You will no doubt be better for it. While there are many ways and methods one can seek clarity, you have to find your own. The only suggestion I will offer is simply to be in the moment and welcome whatever comes to you when you meditate. I can promise, however, that you will eventually develop as a better thinker with clarity and consequently you will become a better manager.

The other physical exercise in my earlier days as a manager was squash. I was an avid squash player in my younger days and I played a lot, even joining a couple of leagues. Being highly competitive, it enabled me to really tune out and release the day's frustration. After a neck operation in 2007, I was told to reconsider playing squash. I have since played socially, but very seldom, as I'm not as fit as I was many years ago. These days, golf is my choice of physical activity.

To recap, I occasionally go to the gym with my son for fitness more than anything else, walk briskly about 5 kms every other day after work, and perform Tai chi after my meditation every morning. In my present position as a consultant and facilitator, this physical exercise allows me to find myself and prepare my day with a positive outlook, which makes all the difference.

I urge you to exercise, no matter what it is you decide to do, for the longevity of your position and for your own well-being. The human body is designed to move, so you should find something to engage in for about an hour a day. I say this for two reasons, one is to stay healthy and the other is to completely switch off from work activities. Remember, you work long hours and need to let go to regenerate and recharge your batteries for the next day. Not only is it great for my physical well-being, but good for my mind. It guarantees optimal performance and your body and mind will thank you for it.

One size doesn't fit all, so find out what works for you even if you only do 30 minutes of workout activity a day, in the morning, afternoon, or evening. We're all different, so as long as you're engaged and committed to looking after your well-being, then that is all that matters.

Diet is another part of life you must make an effort to maintain. Eating the right food at the right time is crucial; it's all about balance. There are many diet available, so find one that works for you. I personally like vegetable greens prepared cold or hot, because green spells growth, and we're growing and learning every day of our lives.

People ask me all the time what motivates me to take good care of myself. They see me drinking funny-tasting green drinks, turning down cookies for a piece of fruit or a coffee latte for the green tea, or getting a little extra sleep at the expense of keeping up with the latest TV drama. If I want to grow old gracefully and be really healthy, I need to be flexible, smart, and able to enjoy physical activity without pain. I know that robust good health won't happen tomorrow unless I do something about it today. I must be proactive and prepare today for tomorrow.

Key Notes

Find a balance between work, health and family life. I consider health to be the most important, because without it you have nothing. It's the cumulative experience of your life, and it's the little things that you do every day that have the biggest impact on your well-being. You can take control of your own health no matter your age, race, sex or current health condition!

The universe will present opportunities at the right time, when your thinking and intentions are aligned. Life is full of adversity and challenges—learn to accept this and allow it to flow as intended. I started using the Serenity Prayer* much later in my career, which enabled me to stay calm when making decisions. Life is simply about timing: being in the right place at the right time. Choose to be positive and thankful for what you have, rather than seeing the glass as half empty.

"Good health is a crown on the head of a well person that only a sick person can see."
~ Robin Sharma

* "Lord, grant me the serenity to accept the things that I cannot change, the strength and courage to change the things that I can, and the wisdom to know the difference."

What is your biggest takeaway from this chapter?

24
The FOON Strategy to Success

One thing you must do as a great manager or leader is to make sure you have enough time to think. You can be busy, but you need time to think. I have used the formula below for many years and have also adopted the 80/20 rule to manage my time more effectively as outlined in my previous chapters. Every day try to spend a third of your time thinking and planning, a third of your time performing your role, and a third of your time coaching and engaging to develop your people. This assists you with time management, communication, and conflict management: the three basic traits of a highly effective person.

My daily personal life is based on the same theory:

- One-third exercise and well-being: one hour of Tai chi and yoga with the 21 Tibetan exercises of the monks, and approximately one hour meditating. That's roughly 2 to 2½ hours each morning looking after my well-being.
- One-third social: catching up with friends, playing golf, etc.
- One-third my time: doing chores like assisting my spouse cleaning the house, walking, playing in the park with my dog, learning to playing the guitar, cooking or watching a movie.

I don't have a time limit, but it works pretty much the same way over the day.

My work life is based on the same strategy:

- One-third exercise and well-being; the same as above. There's no difference between a workday or weekend day; it's the same ritual.
- One-third preparing learning and coaching or developing material.
- One-third preparing for meetings, analyzing and preparation of courses, facilitating/coaching, telephones, emails, etc.

My Strategy

1. **Commitment:** I give 100% to myself and to everything I commit to until I succeed.
2. **Ownership:** I am truly responsible for my actions and outcomes, and own everything that takes place in my work and my life.
3. **Integrity:** I always speak the truth. What I promise is what I deliver.
4. **Excellence:** Good enough isn't. I always deliver products and services of exceptional

quality that add value to all involved for the long term.

5. **Communication:** I speak with purpose and inspire empowering and positive conversation. I greet and say goodbye to people using their name. I always apologize for the upsets first and then look for a solution.

6. **Success:** I totally focus my thoughts, energy, and attention on the successful outcome of my actions. I am a successful person.

7. **Education:** I learn from my mistakes. I consistently continue to learn, grow, and master.

8. **Teamwork:** I am part of a team whether I am facilitating, managing, or coaching for an outcome or goal.

9. **Balance:** I have a balanced approach to life; I know that spiritual, social, physical, and family aspects are just as important as financial and intellectual.

10. **Fun:** I view my life as a journey to be enjoyed and appreciated, and I create an atmosphere of fun and happiness so all around me enjoy it as well.

11. **Consistency:** I consistently strive for clarity and communicate with everyone to achieve growth and success.
12. **Gratitude:** I am a truly grateful person. I say thank you and show appreciation often and in many ways. I consistently catch myself and other people doing things right.
13. **Abundance:** I am an abundant person; I allow abundance in all areas of my life by respecting my own self-worth and that of all others.

This is a very simple strategy. I direct my energy to get a favorable outcome or result most of the time. I also live by the Pareto Principle—the 80/20 rule—meaning that I use 20% of my energy to get 80% of the results, so I do more in less time. Another strategy that I also practice is mindfulness and self-awareness, which allows me to think deeply in the moment, known as "the now" moment. I try to be mindful of everything in the present moment, whether it's walking, eating, or facilitating.

Key Notes
I am thankful I had the strength to endure a somewhat hard life when I began my career 40 years

ago. It gave me a pathway of life experiences, wisdom, skills, and knowledge, and it prepared me for this wonderful journey that I'm currently undertaking. Look after yourself and your well-being, because if you don't, there's no one who will do it for you.

What is your biggest takeaway from this chapter?

25
The Service Money Game
(Financial Management)

I knew you'd be intrigued enough to go straight to this chapter—and frankly I don't blame you. Keep in mind, though, that the two characteristics of a great service manager must be integrated in order for the money game to flow more easily for you.

I am going to start off with the basics. And while this book will serve as a guide, you should always check the brand, segmentation, and global specifications for yourself because targets will differ for every country. The accounting fundamentals and basics will always be similar but not necessarily the goals or targets.

Let me now ask you this: What do you think the main objective of the service department is? Some of you might say profitability, while others may say customer satisfaction or loyalty. The majority I assume is leaning toward a 50/50 balance between the two, right? Please allow me to assist you to increase that 50/50 business balance so that it looks like this:

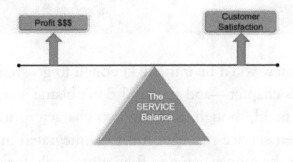

I have said that your people are your greatest assets. Well, guess what? Without the right people we wouldn't be having this conversation. Employee behavior and attitude are key to promoting customer satisfaction, which in turn provides your dealership with loyalty—which generates revenue and profitability. Wow, easy formula. Who says making money is hard? In a perfect world, sure, but we don't live in a perfect world.

Which department do you think makes the greatest amount of gross profit in the dealership? Please take a moment and think about the bigger picture or the bottom line, as they say in the world of money. Take a look below at the revenue pie graph from each department of the dealership. Please bear in mind the department figures could alter one way or another by few percentages.

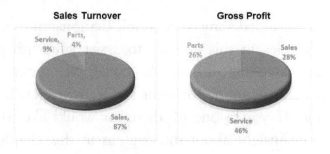

You can see that although the sales department generates the most revenue in the dealership, the service department ultimately generates the most gross profit and that is what drives the business: the healthier the gross, the healthier the bottom line.

Dealership Profitability Indicators

- *Gross Profit = Total Sales less COGS*
  - *Total sales/turnover - Cost of goods sold = Gross Profit*

- *Net Profit = Gross Profit less Expenses*
  - *Gross Profit - Operating expenses = Net Profit*

- *Gross Profit Margin = Total sales/Total Sales less COGS expressed in %*
  - *Total Sales*
    Gross Profit X 100

I have added some very simple demonstrations and examples in this chapter to assist you with your understanding. Financials could be tricky and perhaps daunting for some service managers in the role. If you're one of them, or would like to get more insight about the content in this chapter, I would be more than happy to give you a complimentary coaching session (time pending) for a limited period. Visit my website tonyfoon.com and connect with me for a weekly podcast session.

The philosophy of generating the greatest amount of sales without a basic understanding of accounts may mislead people into focusing on making as much money as they possibly can at the cost of losing loyal customers, good staff, and a proven process. To be truthful, making money is simply about controlling your costs. If costs are controlled, profits will naturally come. The mindset of "the higher the revenue, the greater the profit" isn't necessarily the case all the time. If costs are high, you're working harder perhaps, but maybe not smarter. I would like to prove this very simple theory to you in the following two examples:

Dealership A

Labour Turnover	$55,000
Cost of labour	$15,000
Gross Profit	$40,000
Expenses	$15,500
Direct Profit	$ 24,500

Dealership B

Labour Turnover	$80,000
Cost of labour	$30,000
Gross Profit	$50,000
Expenses	$25,000
Direct Profit	$25,000

Dealership A generates the same profit as Dealership B with fewer sales (turnover) by just controlling one thing, the costs.

After looking at the labor sale and costs in the example above, we can turn to another equation to see the difference in how costs affects the profitability of a dealership.

A routine service has a repair time of 2.5 hours; the price quoted to the customer is based on 2.5 hours of labor. The labor charge-out rate for this dealer is $220 per hour. The technician is paid $20 per hour and takes 2.5 hours to complete the job.

Labor charge	2.5 hours x $220.00 (labor rate) = $550.00
Labor cost	2.5 hours x $20.00 (tech rate) = $ 50.00
Cost of sales % (expressed in %)	$50.00 ÷ $550.00 x 100 = 9.0 %

If the same technician were to work faster than the repair time and completed the job in 2.0 hours, the cost of sales would be affected as shown:

Labor charge	2.5 hours x $220.00 (labor rate) = $550.00
Labor cost	2.0 hours x $20.00 (tech rate) = $ 40.00
Cost of sales % (expressed in a %)	$40.00 ÷ $550.00 x 100 = 7.2 %

You can see from the above example that profitability is all about efficiency (time taken) and effectiveness (adequate in performing tasks).

The only commodity the service department sells is "time," and the cost of labor sales should get the most focus because when the work is performed quickly the greater the profits. Besides the simple example that I just showed, we should look at our cost on a daily basis, especially the variable costs incurred by the business that increase or decrease and are subject to change as the sales level increases and decreases. The cost of sales element is one of the most important elements that a service manager can control and add value to the profitability of the dealership.

Control your costs and your profit will look after itself!

Key Performance Indicators

Let's see what the service has to do to maintain to be profitable and what are some of the Key Performance Indicators (KPI) we should be focusing on.

The service department must do three things well that will make them successful
1. Service the customer needs and wants
2. Retain customers by exceeding their expectations, and
3. Be able to sell every hour that is available and therefore focus on selling time/labor

The last point is paramount in terms of profitability, and the key to service KPI is hourly control. Just like comparing to parts getting the stock levels is key, in sales it's about the value of the inventory/car. Service is all about the hours in a day because we sell nothing else but time.

We have now ascertained the commodity is "time," which is money in the service department. Let's look at how we analyze the hour. The first way is through monitoring the efficiency of the technician and this is done by looking at what hours were sold or invoiced to the customer verses the amount of time that the technician was clocked on.

Efficiency: $$\frac{\textit{Hours Invoiced or Sold}}{\textit{Hours clock}}$$

Benchmark is 100%–110%

This is the relationship between the hours sold and the hours the technician was physically clocked.

The second part of the hour analysis is measuring the productivity. This is done by checking how long the technician was clocked on as compared to the hours that are available for him to work.

Productivity: $$\frac{\textit{Hours clocked}}{\textit{Hours available}}$$

Benchmark is 90%–95%

Selecting the right technician for the job as well as the ability for the technician to complete a job in the timescale recommended by the manufacturer is crucial.

Example: If a technician clocks on for 34 hours and sells or charge out 35 hours, what is his efficiency and productivity expressed in a percentage? Let's dissect and calculate the technician efficiency and productivity below:

- *Available for 38 hours*
- *Clocked hours are 34 hours*
- *Sold hours is 35 hours*

  o *Efficiency:* $\dfrac{35 \text{ hours}}{34 \text{ hours}}$

  o *Productivity:* $\dfrac{34 \text{ hours}}{38 \text{ hours}}$

Prime labor rate (PLR):

- *Prime labor rate:* $\dfrac{\text{Tech weekly salary}}{\text{Hours worked per week}}$

Example: If you paid the technician a weekly salary of $1000 and he worked 38 hours per week you can determine the cost per hour as below.

PLC per hour $\qquad$ <u>*$1000*</u>
$$38hrs = \$26.3$$

Repeat repair

Repeat repairs was one of my pet hates as a manager. The two reasons are the customer has lost faith and will endeavor to vent out in one of those surveys, and the other is that there's a lost opportunity to sell additional revenue. I'm actually losing double by paying the technician for that hour and not getting any revenue from the repairs. Also, there's the matter of lost opportunities to add to profitability for that hour too.

<u>Lost time or non-productive hours</u>

Another pet hate of mine is when time lost and it isn't used to generate revenue. I have paid the technician and the person hasn't able to generate any revenue. In simple terms, lost time is the number of hours bought and not sold or charged to the customers.

Once time is lost you will never be able to recoup it. The best explanation I can offer is to compare this to an airplane ticket sale. There's still an opportunity to sell the ticket because the plane hasn't taken off. Once that plane is on the runaway and ready to take off, there's absolutely no way of selling that ticket; the opportunity is gone forever. Lost time is very much the same comparison: once the day or hour is gone, there's no turning back.

I look at the problem of lost time as a great way for service managers to put their attention on attracting, processing, and retaining more customers. It's your role to monitor the daily bookings and available hours together with the service team and the workshop controller. Remember, the only commodity the service department sells is "time," and if the department isn't using it wisely—the department isn't exceeding customer expectations and best practices processes aren't in place—there's very little chance of increasing profitability.

Service absorption rate

The dealership service absorption rate (expressed in a percentage) is a health check of the dealership, and in essence the stronger or higher this rate is, the better balanced the business. In other words, the operating gross income that the aftersales (parts and service) department generates should be enough to cover the dealership expenses. The greater the amount that expenses can be absorbed by the aftersales department, the better the opportunity and longevity of the dealership.

<u>Gross Profit Service and Parts</u>
Total Dealership Fixed and Semi-fixed Expenses

The ideal target is between 65% to 70%. Let's use the calculation shown below to get a better understanding:

Parts Gross Profit	*$120,000*
Service Gross Profit	*+$160,000*
Total Aftersales Gross Profit	***$280,000***

Fixed & Semi Fixed Expenses Total Dealership is $400,000

Absorption = $250,000 ÷ $400,000 = 70%

Discounting

Discounting has become more common in today's competitive dealership environment. However, the manager must have a process where this is monitored; discounting could prove disastrous if there's no accountability. For example, if a staff member gives a $20 discount to every customer daily and you had an average of say 15 customers a day, over a month the gross figure amounts to $6,150 and over a year this figure is someone else salary. This is what excessive discounting can do to your department.

I used to generate a daily report using codes that monitors everything that was discounted the previous day.

Retail hours per repair order

Retail Hours Per Repair Card	Retail repair order Retail hours sold
Retail repair order	2333
Retail hours sold	3500 = 1.5 hrs

Labor recovery rate

What you actually charged per hour that was sold as opposed to your charge out rate.

Labor sales:	$120,000 (Can RWI)
Hours sold:	560 hrs. (Can RWI)
	= $214 per hour as opposed to your

normal labor, charge out or door rate of say $250 per hour

Benchmark 95% of charge out rate

Break-even analysis

Breakeven is the point in a trading month when gross profit exceeds operating expenses. The goal or target should be around 80% of available working days in month. For example, a month that has 20 working days has a breakeven point at around the 16th day. For a month with 22 working days the breakeven point should be around the 17th/18th day. I shared this with the service department in every dealership, as this is imperative in reaching your targets. Nothing is carved in stone especially when you're in a team environment and people are incentivized in reaching targets.

Please allow me to share my experience with you about a workshop controller/manager that I worked with. This particular gentleman was so narrowed minded that if the allocated budget hours were achieved for the day, he would profusely object to taking in any additional work regardless. He was so oblivious to the fact that we sold "time" in the workshop (because the previous service manager booked in work by the number of cars per day, rather than available hours and was not transparent with him). I had a mission coaching him about financials and changing his mindset as to how the department sold hours/time and the more "time" we sell the more revenue for everyone including him. It's the old scenario, you only know what you know, and unfortunately, he did not know better after all these years.

Average labor sales per repair order
Total labor sales/Number of Repair Order

Example:
Average Labor Sales per Repair Order

Total labor sales: <u>*$3500*</u>
Number of Repair Order: *20*   =   *$175 per Repair Order*

Average hours per repair order
Productive clocked hours/Number of Repair Order

Example:
Average Hours per Repair Order

Productive clocked hours: <u>*47*</u> *hours*
Number of Repair Order: *20*   =   *2.35hrs per Repair Order*

Labor Sales Mix

A large part of service profitability is the labor sales mix, which is the difference between achieving your monthly budget and KPI. One example I can share is that in one of my previous roles I was asked to analyze two dealerships that had the same brand. However, one of the dealerships was significantly larger than the other. Given that the larger dealership had more expenses, but also more turnover, the smaller one was generating more profit at the end of the month. To be fair, this wasn't due to the level of management though the manager of the larger dealership should have been proactive in analyzing the result: An examination of six months of financial data revealed that the labor sales mix was different between the two dealerships. Taking the data and comparing like for like, I noticed the gross profits of the labor mix between the two dealerships was a major factor and discovered that the difference was in the way the work sales mix was booked.

The larger dealership was booking everything, filling the day or hours with whatever bookings that was scheduled, where the smaller one was smart in what it filled its day with, taking into account all things being equal and keeping as close to the benchmark of the labor sales mix KPI below.

Retail/labor mix expressed at 70%; that's the winner, as it is your bread and butter
Warranty/labor mix expressed at 20%; we all know that's not real in this world
Internal/labor mix expressed at 10%; unless the charge is the same as the retail rate, it will always not be a priority to do. In saying that, the used car department is your largest or most consistent customer, so look after them as customers.

Labor Sales per Service Adviser

Comparing repair order of your team is an important measure, but the focus should be directed to labor sales. This is an element that the service adviser has direct control and influence. This should be monitor on a daily basis for coaching purposes.

Parts-to-Labor Ratio

Parts-to-labor ratio is the ratio of labor sales to parts sold over a certain period. For example, parts to labor ratio of 0.8:1 means that for every dollar of labor sale that the dealership earns, it sells 80 cents worth of parts. If parts-to-labor ratio is high this normally indicates that the service is charging too little for labor.

Key KPI to monitor
<u>Monthly:</u>
Labor Recovery Rate
Labor Gross Profit
Labor Cost of Sales
Customer Appointment Rate

<u>Weekly:</u>
Lost Hours
Departmental Expenses
Parts to-Labor
Sales Mix
NPS Customer Retention

<u>Daily</u>
Productivity
Efficiency

Key Notes

At this point, I assume that you understand the following basic accounting structure of the service department. Here's a brief summary:

- Turnover or sales revenue:
  - o Income generated from the sale of goods, in this case, labor or time.

- Costs:
  - o This is the associated cost that we paid to have the above sale, known also as COS or COGS (cost of sale or cost of goods sold). This is the cost of what you paid the technicians to generate the sale (labor/time)

- Gross Profit:
  - o This is the amount of money that you have accumulated from the sale as a result of taking your cost into account.

- Expenses:
  - o This includes all departmental expenses including variable expenses and fixed-

group expenses: salaries to operating expenses along with other expenses.

- Net Profit:
  - This is known as the bottom line and is what is deposited in the bank at the end, all things being equal. Calculated by deducting the expenses from the gross profit.

" Planning is looking at the future and doing something about it today. Plans are nothing, planning is everything!"
~ Alan Lakein

What is your biggest takeaway from this chapter?

26
Emotional Intelligence
(It's a Must Have)

Have you ever been in a situation where you had to work with someone you report to who screams, belittles, and verbally abuses you to get a message across? I feel confident in saying that if you've ever been treated in this manner, the experience made you feel worthless. This has also happened to me, and on one occasion that I recall a display of arrogant, ignorant, and obnoxious behavior got me to walk out of a boardroom manager meeting. My takeaway from that experience is simple and direct: No one should ever talk to anybody in a condescending way because it's not professional, it's disrespectful, and it's unethical. Such rude behavior was the norm many years ago when I started out as a young service manager in the 1990s, but I can assure you that things have changed for the simple reason that no one wants to engage with people who have any of the negative characteristics I've just described. I'm sure you've all heard the expression "people don't leave companies, they leave managers." Understanding emotional intelligence helps explain why this happens.

What do we know about emotional intelligence (EI)? First of all, EI—sometimes referred to as EQ (emotional quotient)—is different from understanding a person's intelligence quotient (IQ). Many years ago, it was often assumed by people from an older generation of managers that IQ was central to understanding a person's suitability for getting hired. Keep in mind that a person's IQ is still important but has become less relevant when compared to the emphasis placed on EQ. Why the change? Well, you simply have to take into account the generational diversity of the workforce in our society today. People want to be more connected; therefore, we have to adapt to the tenor of the day. In some ways, this is a good thing because people learn to work with each other as a team as opposed to working individually. Let me now go into more detail on the difference between IQ and EQ.

IQ is how we measure someone's reasoning ability or how well we can use logic to answer questions. If you have a low IQ, you will likely struggle with some things; if you have a high IQ, you're considered very intelligent. Frankly speaking, I'm not exactly sure how true this is now, because in my experience people with a high IQ don't always perform at a high level. When I began investigating the reason why this is so, I discovered that high IQ people aren't necessarily people who understand the nuances and subtleties of emotions, and although they possess intelligence when it comes to knowledge and logic, they would struggle with empathy when working with others.

EQ concerns understanding your own emotions and how you react empathetically to other people's emotions and is now a required measurement tool that managers are expected to master. Many years ago I attended a conference where an activity on IQ and EQ characteristics was undertaken. The question concerned what we thought about a person who had a high IQ and a person with a high EQ, and of the two who would be the candidate most likely to be a high performer at certain tasks that involve knowledge and emotions. Most participants who were at the conference including me made a decision that the person with the high IQ should have done better at the job. To our amazement, we were surprised that it was the person with the high EQ who would perform better at the job. The reasoning behind this is that the majority of people with a high IQ tend to be low at emotional contact. The person with the high EQ did better at connecting with people working as a team and therefore was rated as a better overall performer at the job.

I hope you can see why this is such an important skill to learn. In order to be successful, a high level of IQ *and* EQ are needed. I will now share a personal experience that explains why understanding EQ is necessary in order to be a great service manager.

Living in South Africa for the most part of my life many years ago, and from an Asian culture, I was bought up with minimum emotional contact. My parents were working all day and late at night to raise my siblings and me. It was all about work and no play and there was very little time for us to be connected emotionally. From my childhood days it was always about working hard at what we do, and as I mentioned in my earlier chapters, we were told that kids should be seen and not heard. This made me very shy when I was growing up, and it also disconnected from being emotional. It was only until I went to boarding school in my teenage years that I fully experienced emotions. In my earlier days as a manager my mentality of management was about catching people doing the wrong things.

A few years ago, I went to another conference on emotional intelligence, as I was intrigued to find out more what EQ was all about. The lady who was presenting said that EQ is a skill that all managers in the future need to possess. I thought she was joking and don't know what she was talking about because I thought managers just needed to be resilient and to ensure that employees did their jobs properly with no emotions attached. As I begin to mature in my role, I soon realized that you had to control your emotions in order to get the best out of your employees. Through learning and practicing this skill, and talking and reacting to people emotions, I soon noticed there was a change in the way they responded to me: They reacted in a more positive manner.

Let's look at some examples of emotionally connecting with people. They seem very confident in what they do and how they look and present themselves. They also seem in my view more positive about life in general. They are smiling for the most part and don't seem to sweat the small stuff. They appear very calm when making decisions and nothing seems to faze them. I didn't understand as a young service manager when everything was about me doing the things right and catching people doing the wrong things. A large part of my understanding of EQ was engaging in a mentor. Much to his credit he taught me an abundance of information regarding emotional intelligence, which led me to investigate this further. I subsequently noticed that it was more to just being able to understand your own and as well as other people's emotions. It was quite fascinating, and it led me to embark onto this journey to find out about this topic, which has opened the door for future learning. I would now like to further share with you my experiences when I started to learn more about emotional intelligence.

One thing that was fascinating was that you could actually read body language. I was so intrigued by this that I later attended an entire course on body language and started reading books on body language. One particular book that I was reading was called *What Every Body Says* by Joe Navarra, an ex-FBI interrogator. Navarra discussed facial expressions, body posture, hand and leg posture, and other interesting body cues. I was able to apply what I learned from this book during my training sessions.

A fascinating point I noticed about my mentor was, when I was talking, he would listen to me with great intent and undivided attention, which made me feel really good. At the end of every session he always asked how I felt. At that stage, I was forming my own opinions about my mentor because that was a sign of emotional intelligence. He understood my feelings and thoughts and showed empathy to ensure that we parted on a positive note.

Another noticeable behavior about people who possess high emotional intelligence is that they aren't scared to ask you something that they don't know the answers to. A very simple example that has always stayed with me occurred when my wife and I were dating. She asked me if she should put milk and sugar in the Chinese green tea before she actually drank it. I thought that was pretty funny because most people I know drink green tea without sugar or milk. In her defense she never had green tea prior to meeting me; she assumed that it was the same as black tea. It wasn't the question she asked, but *how* she asked it that made the difference without any embarrassment while showing a level of openness to learning about different cultures.

For a long time, I had to learn how to control my feelings, to learn how to deal with people without pushing and pulling them with force. Put simply, I learned how to interact with care and empathy. Learning about EQ made me aware how I was dealing with my own emotions and subsequently how to react with solutions in a calm and professional manner.

All of this occurred at about the same time I started meditate, which also put me in a positive state of mind. I became more confident, and in some ways had more clarity and openness in the way I looked and thought about things. I must admit it took me awhile before I absorbed and digested this new way of managing people. My newfound realization came down to this: People don't care about how much you know; they want to know how much you care.

This is one of the most important skills for managers to learn, as it will help you to be successful in connecting and engaging with your people. Both IQ and EQ play a role in how successful we become. The only difference now is the world has become more connected, which means that EQ offers a larger part in the way we manage our employees. My opinion is that every student can learn no matter how intelligent, but not every student can have an emotional connection. I'm hoping you will start learning about EQ so that you can be more successful in the future.

Key Notes

Communicating with emotional intelligence:

- Allows you to connect with your staff
- Allows you to be more self-aware of your own emotions and therefore helps you to control your reactions
- Allows you to experience positivity, which helps you and others around you to think and perform better
- Allows you to be able to make better decisions in challenging situations
- Can alter your attitude in a positive manner (because of your controlled emotions)
- Allows you to be a much calmer person
- Means you can expect a highly productive team

Learning this skill will take time, patience, and practice, but you will soon discover that mastering emotional intelligence is helpful for your own well-being, and in your role as a manager.

What is your biggest takeaway from this chapter?

27
Make Warranty Claims Your Business

I fell into a warranty clerk position by default when I was working as a service advisor for a prestige dealership many years ago. It was probably one of the best things that ever happened. It gave me an understanding of warranty claims and what is involved in terms of policies and process. My outlook on being warranty specialist is simple: It is 20% of your business and could be 80% of your headache if processes and procedures are not followed.

As a franchise dealer, you're obligated to perform warranty claims on the brands you represent, so you ought to understand the process. This is no different to the other sales mix except that you have more work to do for less revenue. That's the cost of representing a brand that keeps you employed.
I know many service managers who aren't involved with warranty claims because they either don't have the time, or are simply not interested. To be blunt, if your salary depended on a warranty claim, would you be interested? The bad news is that warranty claims are part of your salary because if a claim is charged back due to missing parts, or a work order is misfiled, that comes out of your department's profitability for the month, which impacts the overall bottom line.

What if I said you had an audit and the extrapolation was a significant amount, and that was part of your commission base, e.g., 5%–10% of the total extrapolation amount. Would you get involved then? The best service managers run their departments like their own business. You must be trained on policies and procedure, but to coach your staff moving forward, remember that you're fully accountable for your department.

When I was a service manager, I made it my business to know all about warranty claims in the event that I had to carry the torch until a solution was found. I was in a precarious situation when my warranty clerk, after repeated warnings about his need to do the right thing, didn't follow the processes, and so he was asked to leave. I was left with no choice but to take on warranty claims until another person was found. Can you imagine if I ignored warranty claims for three weeks or possibly longer until a replacement was found? With most manufacturers allowing only a 14-day deadline on claim submissions, what would have happened?

I recently contracted my services to a dealership to do their warranty claims for three weeks, as their warranty clerk was away for an operation. Two things set off my alarm bells. First, what succession plan did the dealer or manager have in place? In other words, why was no one trained for this position as a backup? For all other positions in the dealership, there was someone to step in if a person wasn't available. Second, as a service manager, I'm required to learn all about warranty claims in the event that this scenario occurs, which includes looking at the work orders, transmitting the claims, and ensuring the processes are in place. Instead, they hired my services as a warranty clerk. I'm not complaining, as it was additional income, but this would have undoubtedly affected the department's profitability.

The point I'm making is that this manager should have been the one carrying out the warranty claim, not me. Take the time to learn, because you might be faced with the same scenario. It's common and it happens, so be proactive and get involved, even if it means having a one-on-one training session with the manufacturer. They will always assist if you show initiative.

Key Notes
Have a backup warranty clerk as part of your succession planning; this could simply be an

internal person. Get people trained in warranty claims even if you have to invest in the training. You won't regret it. Believe me!

Make warranty claims your business, because great service managers ensure they don't have to depend on anyone else. Unless you're the chef of a restaurant, don't invest in the business, because if the chef walks out and you can't cook, guess what? You're out of business.

What is your biggest takeaway from this chapter?

28
The Habits of a Highly Effective Service Manager

Eight Habits of a Productive Manager

Habit 1: Focus on the important things

The first thing to do is to slice and dice everything that's unimportant. Whenever I go to my work desk, I write down a list of things to do for the day. I then evaluate which are the most important by circling them and ranking them in order of importance. Do things that make a difference every day. There's no point in doing something unimportant!

My most important tasks are the ones that bring me closest to the completion of my goals. For example, working on my book allows me to connect with more people and achieve my end vision of enabling those people to reach their highest potential and live their best life. While other tasks also help me progress toward my goals, they're not as effective as working on my book at this point.

Habit 2: Allocate breaks

Discovering what time your mojo peaks during the day is very important. Some people are more productive in the afternoon, while others are more productive in the morning, like myself.

Rest is important. I space breaks in between work to catch up on emails, exercise, read a book, go for a walk, see a friend, take a short nap, and so on. I call this "me time." Whenever you feel unproductive, throw in a quick break. Walk away from the desk, have a toilet break, or talk to a colleague about work, anything. And remember to take your lunch away from your desk.

Habit 3: Remove distractions

Emails are probably my biggest distraction. I have learned to deal with this by only checking them on a break. Observe what else is distracting you. How can you remove it? Experiment by working in different places and trying something different.

Habit 4: Tap into your inspiration

I can't stress how important this is for maximizing output—your inspiration is your key. For example, an inspired writer will continually write material that everyone wants to read, and a highly inspired musician writes one song after another.

I fully grasped the impact of inspiration when I started my journey. I realized that during the times I was inspired, work was simply effortless. Now, when I get up at the crack of dawn, I'm inspired, and when writing this book, the words flow easily like I'm having a conversation.

Find what motivates you and use that to drive you. My biggest inspiration is seeing others achieve their highest potential and living their best lives. My aim has always been to set people up for success.

Habit 5: Create barriers

A great thing about our world today is that it's easier than ever to reach out to someone. Everyone is just an SMS, phone call, email, or even a Facebook message away. At the same time, the world has become a very distracting place to live, which sucks energy from doing what matters … to you. Sometimes you need to put barriers in place. Otherwise you won't get anything done.

When I'm busy coaching or facilitating, I switch off my phone and only check it at the end of the day to return messages. I continue to get regular emails, but won't respond to them unless they require a reply of one or two words. It's not about being difficult, it's about focusing on what matters to me and creating real value for others with my undivided attention. As the old saying goes, "sometimes you have to be cruel to be kind."

Habit 6: Take advantage of time pockets

Time pockets are when you have a few moments to spare. They usually occur when waiting for people, commuting, or walking from one place to another. Maximize them by reading books, planning, etc. You will be amazed at how much can be done in just a short amount of time! For example, I largely work from my home office now, but when I commute, I take every opportunity to maximize my time and I'm highly productive during these time pockets.

Habit 7: Set timelines

Timelines are a fundamental productivity habit. If you don't set a timeline, you can take forever to complete what you're doing. If you set a timeline of two weeks, you'll take two weeks. The key is to be disciplined.

I do regular goal setting to maximize my output. Be clear on what you want to achieve (Habit 1), then set your timelines accordingly. What do you want to finish this month? Make a realistic target and go for it. This is the 30/30/1 formula for managing your time that I spoke about earlier in my chapters.

Habit 8: Automate everything possible

Technology today has made automation possible for a lot of things we do. Use it or lose it. If you get a feeling of déjà vu when doing something, that's a cue to automate that item. The reason I love Apple products is because I can sync all my devices. The result is that I'm always on top of everything.

The Pareto Principle (80/20 Rule)

I would like to reiterate the power of applying the 80/20 rule to your life. In any given situation, 80% of the results are from 20% of the cause, or 80% of the results come mostly from 20% of people. In the end, the rule allows you to achieve more with less energy. It gives you extraordinary results with little action.

Apply the 80/20 Rule in three steps:

- Identify your 80/20 destination—what truly matters to you. What are your goals and dreams in this world? Eighty percent of your goals should be generated by twenty percent of your efforts.
- Identify your 80/20 route, applying the "less is more" theory.
- Identify your 80/20 action; always use 20% energy to get 80% of the results.

Key Notes

Timing is everything in what you do. Apply the 80/20 three-step approach to your life. Start with a small part, then move on from there. The sky is the limit! (The mantra on my website!)

"Every dream starts small. But you need to start. Today."
~ Robin Sharma

What is your biggest takeaway from this chapter?

Conclusion

You are the master of your own destiny. Your future career tomorrow depends on what you decide to do today. Your career is in your hands. I have shared with you my experiences from three different continents worldwide and maintain that the service management role isn't difficult, provided you have the skills and knowledge to perform well in the role. What is difficult is the juggling of personalities, as no two persons are alike. We're all different and therefore finding a style from my book or your own style is crucial if you want to succeed further in your career. It's virtually impossible for me to recall all incidents or situations from my career when writing this book. In saying that, I'm more than happy to assist you in any way I can by asking you to please email me your queries and I will share more ideas and knowledge with you personally and individually.

After many years in a management position, I always wanted to be able to pass my wisdom and experiences to others. During 2009, in my last role in management, I decided to pursue further studies to obtain a training certificate and start committing to the long-life journey of a coach and facilitator. Through this and my networks, many opportunities have come my way and I have seized those opportunities to be in the position I'm in today. It's fair to say that I have created my own luck. The opportunities that I have encountered along the way has inevitably allowed many other doors to open for me. As I've always maintained, sometimes in life you need to accept challenges and seize opportunities that are presented to you. As the saying goes "nothing ventured, nothing gained."

Challenges will always be daunting, but unless you try, you will never know your true potential. I have never been a facilitator in my life, but my inspiration to be one had me pursuing this journey. I've have never looked back since. Sure, I had people who doubted me, and I can still remember some people who tried to discourage me, but unless you give yourself the opportunity to try, you're never going to know. Remember, there's only one of you in this universe, so I have maintained the philosophy that what other people say and think about me is none of my business. You have to start with a goal in mind and be prepared to continue to stay the course to achieve this goal and to persevere no matter the challenges that may lie ahead. You're the only person who can imagine your dream and take the steps to achieve it.

I would like you to take these few principles that I have adopted many years in the role. They will prove to be vital for your success:

Know what you don't know

- As a leader, you're a generalist; hire the right people.
- Rely on their skills, to make your role easier and to delegate more effectively.

Resist the (What's in it for me) WIIFM syndrome

- Don't beat your own drum (no one cares).
- People don't care about what you know; people want to know how much you care.

Never underestimate the competition

- Prepare, plan, and always be proactive in your approach.

You're only as good as your employees

- Always treat your staff exactly as you want them to treat your best customers.
- Listen to everyone's ideas because even the car detailer can have the best idea.

Be passionate about learning

- Constantly seek knowledge and be curious all the time; keep asking questions.
- Learn something new every day; that's 365 things that you can learn in a year.

Don't expect your staff to do anything that you would not do. This book was written to guide you in how to avoid making the same or silly mistakes that I made as a service and operations manager in the industry. It will enable you to do better job and enhance your skills to be more successful than I was in my career. I hope that you will pass on your wisdom and knowledge that you have learned to others because the Chinese proverb says: *"That the best way to learn is to teach and the best way to teach is to learn."* You must and should never stop learning as long as you are alive.

Key point:

If you prepare, plan, and are proactive in your approach to what you want, you will succeed. As the ancient Chinese proverb states: "All the flowers of tomorrow are in the seeds of today." The harder you work, the luckier you get, and the more you prepare, the better the desired outcome. The Chinese general Sun Tzu says, "Every battle is won before it is fought." Yes. It is all about planning. Always.

I thank you for reading this book. I hope that it has assisted you to be the best that you can be. I sincerely wish you greatness and success in your pursuit to be a successful service/operations manager for many years to come. I will leave you with this thought that there's only one of you, everyone else is taken: Be yourself.

"If you can dream it, you can do it" -- Walt Disney

The Art of Successful Service Management

- 288 -

About Tony Foon

Tony's experience comes from being in the trenches. In every position, from apprentice to general aftersales manager, he was consistently recognized for achieving the highest levels of performance. He is in his 40th year of doing business and has spent the greater part of that time successfully training and mentoring clients in the art of management and leadership

He is a mentor and coach to many frontline service advisors and managers in various parts of the world ranging from South Africa, Southeast Asia, New Zealand, Canada, and Australia.

Most who experience Tony's training say it is the most practical, realistic, and easy-to-understand service training ever. Tony's style of delivery and coaching is more consultative and collaborative, which has been very well received from participants who say they prefer this to the style of "telling."

He uses best practice methodologies to customize learning initiatives to develop people and improve their performance. His key skills and strengths are leadership development programs including employee engagement, emotional intelligence, communication skills, customer service skills, work life balance, conflict resolution, and time management. His practical and interactive training sessions use real-life situations and experiences that develop initiative and resilience.

He has led and developed key personnel within company management structures, while maintaining his "customer is key" philosophy.

Through his methods and mentoring, he has successfully managed to instill a sense of pride, passion, and devotion to excellence among staff members, thereby creating an environment that allows for continued success and progression.

In 2003, Tony was Service Manager of the Year at DaimlerChrysler in Australia. In 2004, he attained a Certification in Management at the University of Canberra and the Australian Institute of Management. He was also recognized for academic excellence in Management and Organizational Development in Theory and Practices, Marketing Strategy, Financial Business and Human Resources Management. In 2006, he was promoted to General Service Manager, overseeing seven dealerships and twelve franchises. In 2007 and 2008, under Tony's leadership, the Audi Centre Canberra Service Department received the Dealer of the Year award. In 2009, he was nominated for the Top 5 Mercedes Benz Service Managers of the Year.

HOW TO CONTACT TONY

URL: tonyfoon.com

Strategy Session:
tonyfoon.com/resources/free-strategy-session/

Email: tony@tonyfoon.com